# Muslims in America
# Opportunities &
# Challenges

Foreword by
Sulayman Nayang

Asad Husain
John E. Woods
Javeed Akhter

POSITION PAPER TWO

International Strategy and Policy Institute
Chicago, Illinois

First Published 1996

ISBN # 0-9647204-1-8

Printed in the United States of America

## Dr. Fazlur Rahman Khan
### *(1934-1996)*

This ISPI publication is dedicated to the memory of the president of ISPI and our dear friend Dr. Fazlur Rahman Khan.

*May Allah bless his soul for his efforts in spreading a better understanding of Islam in North America.*

# ACKNOWLEDGEMENT

The Executive Committee and the Board of Directors of ISPI would like to acknowledge IQRA' International Educational Foundation, Skokie IL for its time and effort in production and publication of this book.

# CONTENTS

FOREWORD
*Prof. Sulayman S. Nayang*
ix


A BRIEF HISTORY AND DEMOGRAPHICS
OF MUSLIMS IN THE UNITED STATES
*Prof. Asad Husain*
19


IMAGINING AND STEREOTYPING ISLAM
*Prof. John Woods*
45


MUSLIMS IN THE USA
OPPORTUNITIES AND CHALLENGES:
A PROACTIVE VISION
*Javeed Akhter M.D.*
79


ABOUT ISPI
93


ABOUT THE AUTHORS
94

You are indeed the best community
That has ever been brought forth for mankind
You enjoin the doing of what is right
And forbid the doing of what is wrong
And believe in God.

Qur'an 3:110

# FOREWORD

American Muslims are now counted as part of a faith community whose growing numbers could place them in the next century as the second largest religious community in the country. This development in American religious and cultural history has serious implications for both the Muslim and the average American who is not Muslim. What are these implications and how are the Muslims and their leaders dealing with these challenges? This book, which is the fruit of the labors of members of the board of the International Strategy and Policy Institute (ISPI) based in Chicago, Illinois, is the result of serious research and soul-searching efforts to grapple with the problems of religious and cultural adjustment for the diverse body of Muslims now living within the borders of the United States of America. Its publishers are the members and leaders of one of the very few, if not the only functioning, Muslim think tanks that are beginning to carve a niche for themselves in the American political and cultural landscape. In a country where there are at least 40,000 think tanks, if one were to start counting from the mom and pop operations to the giant think tanks like the Rand Corporation, the Heritage Foundation, the American Enterprise Institute and the Brookings Institution, the Muslim organization responsible for the production of this volume is presently a small but growing institute based in Chicago, Illinois. Its objectives consist of making known to the wider American society the aspirations and dreams of Muslims living and creating within the American civilization. Committed to the preservation of their religion in the society, and equally determined to carve a place in the American sun for themselves and their descendants, these Muslims who are now trying to disseminate more reliable and non-prejudicial information about Americans of the Islamic faith strongly believe their think tank is an important instrument of self-affirmation. But before one can elaborate on the need for such an institution and the role and place it holds in the dissemination of more accurate data about the Muslims and their communities across the United States of America, let us answer briefly and in passing the question: who are the Muslims in the United States of America and, if they are immigrants, where did they come from in the Muslim World?

According to available research data, the Muslim community could trace its history back to pre-Columbian times. Some of the limited evidence gathered by earlier scholars are presented in the essay written by Professor Asad Husain of the Northeastern Illinois University at Chicago, Illinois. The second phase in the history of this world religion in the US goes back to the times of slavery when, according to Allan Austin, author of *African Muslims in Ante Bellum America.*, at least ten per cent of the slaves brought over here from the African continent were Muslims. Some of them were well known to men like Theodore Dwight, the Secretary of the American Ethnological Society in the mid-nineteenth century, who devoted a significant amount of time and energy collecting materials and documenting the lives and times of Muslim slaves in America. In this brief foreward one could identify a few for the benefit of the readers of this volume. Perhaps the most widely celebrated case was that of Job Ben Solomon (Ayub ibn Sulayman Diallo), an African Muslim prince from Bondu in what is present day Guinea-Conakry, who was captured and sold to slave traders in colonial America. He was freed later by an English officer of the British Navy and returned to Africa. There were other cases and the stories of Yarrow Mamouth of Georgetown, Omar Ibn Said in Fayetteville, North Carolina and Abdur Rahman from Guinea-Conakry ought to be recounted over and over again for the better enlightenment of the American Muslim and his or her neighbor.

Of these three better known slaves who maintained or

tried to maintain their Islamic faith, only two of them made it back to Africa. The first one, who is know in the literature as the "Fortunate Slave", went back to his home country of Guinea - Conakry. The second one was Abdur Rahman, another prince who became a slave in Natchez, Mississippi in the United States of America, but was manumitted thanks to the intervention of the Sultan of Morocco. According to the sources of the time, he was able to secure the freedom of his wife but not his children. He reluctantly left the US bound for Guinea by way of Liberia. Unfortunately, he died enroute to his home for reunion after long separation from relatives and friends.

Besides the two slaves who were fortunate enough to secure their freedom and return to their country, there were two others who managed to get their freedom but after old age had already set in. The first one was Omar ibn Said, who fled to Fayetteville, North Carolina and was manumitted by his master many years after his arrival in that town. The second one was Yarrow Mamouth (correctly known as Yoro Mahmoud), perhaps the oldest American ever to live in these United States of America, according to the records left behind by the nineteenth century American artist Vincent Peil who immortalized Yarrow by drawing a portrait of him and describing his encounter with this aged African in his diary.

The third phase in the history of Muslim immigration to the United States of America began in the post civil war period when a wave of Arab immigration from the Ottoman empire began to settle along the eastern seaboard and into the heartland of America in the mid-west. Many of these immigrants came here in the hope of striking it rich and then return home to enjoy their fortune from America. Destiny ruled otherwise, and most of them ended up marrying American brides or ordered a spouse from the familiar surroundings of Mount Lebanon or Syria. It was out of this mixed bag of dreams about America and myths about returning home after making it that combined to lay the moral and psychological foundation of these early groups of immigrants. In retrospect, one can argue that though "the myth of return" still enjoys some support among more recent immigrants, the growing assimilation of most Muslims of the second and third generations has made it more and more imperative for the Muslims to build up structures and develop the mechanisms of self development and self-affirmation. The think tank that sponsors this volume is setting the precedent for the coming generations of Muslims who are presently toiling in America's academic vineyards for their training and careers.

Indeed the fourth phase in the development of Islamic structures and institutions in America began with the coming of the Muslim students in the post war period. Attracted to the halls of learning of the American society, and determined to succeed by all legitimate means, many of these young men and women who came here returned home laden with the golden fleece of American higher education. There were however others who for a variety of reasons decided to settle down permanently in the US. Some of these individuals were the victims of political circumstances in the Muslim World and they decided it was politically prudent to make the US their permanent home. Yet, there were others for whom conjugal entanglements played a far more serious part than anything else in their decision to stay here for good. Regardless of how and why they stayed here, the fact remains that those who embraced the philosophy of the Muslim Student Association (MSA), would later graduate and settle in America. Many of these generations of Muslim immigrants graduated from colleges and universities and then became Muslim professionals in the larger society. They are the founding fathers of such Muslim organizations like the Islamic Society of North America (ISNA), the Islamic Circle of North America (ICNA), the Association of Muslim Social Scientists (AMSS), the Association of Muslim Scientists and Engineers (AMSE) and the Islamic Medical Association (IMA). These organizations have created a significant presence among Muslims who are willing to come out of the social and political closet and affirm their faith and their rituals in their workplaces and in those parts of the Public Square where they encounter strangers who are as committed to their faith as those Muslims willing to do *dawah* (proselytization efforts) in America's public fora.

In our brief review of the history of the Muslims of the United States of America, we would be in error if we fail to show how the third and the fourth phases have together created the mental and physical spaces for the planting of Islam among the native-born citizens of the country. Since the death of Muhammad Alexander Russell Webb early in this century, the numbers of indigenous Muslims have increased significantly over the last ninety years. This fascination with Islam and the dramatic rise in the total number of Muslims among American citizens, have been traced to conversion and natural birth among the immigrants and the converts. These Muslims who are now seen by society as "converts" would prefer to be called "reverts" instead. The increase in their numbers is largely due to the efforts of Shaykh Daud Faisal, an African-American musician who claimed a Moroccan father and a West Indian mother. Shaykh Daud and his spouse played a key role in the dissemination of Islam among blacks living in the New York / New Jersey area. Their *dawah* (proselytization efforts) work among the non-Muslims led to the conversion of many members of the African-American community. In addition to the activities of the Shaykh from the State Street Mosque in Brooklyn, New York, there were also the efforts of the Nation of Islam to circulate some understanding of Islamic concepts no matter how distorted they appeared to their Muslim contemporaries in the 1930s. As history would have it, the efforts of the late Elijah Muhammad have done more for the multiplication of Muslim numbers than any *dawah* from other groups of Muslims in the country. With the accession of Imam W.D. Muhammad to the top position of the inherited Nation of Islam, dramatic changes began to take place within this powerful black movement.

Imam Mohammad has made history in his successful

transformation of the Nation of Islam without any violence or major disturbances among his followers. By focusing on the spiritual elevation of his followers and by urging them to take responsibility for their spiritual growth and development through the institutionalization of autonomy among the heretofore dependent *masajid* (mosques) scattered across the US, he opened the floodgates of spiritual challenges to his followers and thus enabled them to build individual and collective bridges to the immigrant Muslims at home and the overseas Muslims in the Old World. It is indeed the individual and collective legacies of Shaykh Daud and Honorable Elijah Muhammad that created the intellectual, moral and psychological conditions for other Islamic movements to emerge out of the African-American communities. The Darul Islam Movement, the Islam Brotherhood, Inc., in New York, the Islamic Party of North America headed by Hamid Muzaffrudin, the Hanafi group headed by Abdul Khaalis, and all other smaller and splinter groups were either inspired by Shaykh Daud Faisal or were at one time members of the Nation of Islam.

The history of Islam in the US would be incomplete if we fail to add the role and place of the followers of the Sufi orders in the country. Like the Islamic schools of jurisprudence, the Sufi orders were also brought to the United States of America by the migrating Muslims from the Old World. Centered on the mystical dimensions of the Islamic experience and usually quiet about their activities, this aspect of Islam has been most appealing to Americans of European ancestry. Some have suggested that the political quietism among Sufi orders has been one of the reasons for its attraction to this segment of the Muslim Community in the US. Those who make such statements are usually driven to this conclusion after they have compared and contrasted the manner in which many blacks as opposed to most white Muslims in the US., have used Islam as an ideological weapon against racial discrimination in the society. True or false, this perception is shared by both Muslims and non-Muslims in America. Indeed, it is an important point to be registered by members of think-tanks like the publishers of this volume. Such divergent views of American society and such differential attitudes towards the political system and the assimilation of Muslims in the larger society, could easily replicate the divisions within the larger society among the racially diversified membership of the emerging Muslim community. Strategic thinking and planning among the Muslims, one must add, could help obviate this potentially major problem. One group that is trying to build a bridge of brotherhood and sisterhood among the multiracial American Muslim community through its annual Powow and Quran Intensive Program is the Darul Islam community based in Abiqui in New Mexico.

But lest we misspeak about the divergent opinions on and the differential attitudes towards American culture among the different Muslim groups, whether black or white or native-born or immigrant, let it be noted here that the Sufi movement among Muslims is color-blind. Its adherents are drawn from all over the Muslim World. There are advocates from Asia who hailed from areas where the Chishtiya, the Qadriya, the Naqshbandiya, the Nimatullah, and many others located in the Middle East and central Asia. There are also branches of these orders in Africa, where splinter groups have formed over the centuries since the arrival of Sufism in this part of the world. In the special case of the United States of America, the Sufi movement has brought elements from almost all parts of Darul Islam. They have in fact taken three different directions. There are those Sufi groups from West Africa, especially the Muridiyya and Tijanniyya orders whose followers from Senegal and the Sahelian region of West Africa have become active peddlers and traders in the New York area. Their activities in Manhattan and Harlem have been documented by local New York media. The other trend among the Sufi orders is the attempt to create small communities on the West Coast or along the eastern seaboard of the country. The third trend is the attempt of major Sufi groups like the Naqshbandiya to mainstream themselves among the non-Sufi

Muslim majority in the country. These efforts at planting the seeds of Sufism in American society and within the traditionally non-Sufi Muslim families have significant implications for the future of Islam in America. The publishers of this volume which seeks to educate Americans about the Muslim community would need to pay attention to the emerging dialogue between the Sufi orders and their followers on the one hand, and the non-Sufis in the country on the other. Even if there are no dialogues in the Old World, the common destiny of the Muslim community in this country has made it categorically clear that such dialogues between Sufis and non-Sufis are necessary.

Another area of life for the Muslim leadership and strategic thinkers is the assimilation of and the extension of goodwill to the Native Americans and the Hispanic Americans who have decided voluntarily to join the ranks of the Islamic community in the US. As of this writing, there are hundreds if not thousands of members of these American minority communities who are now counted among American Muslims. In order for the Muslims in the US to make a powerful impression on the larger society, their leadership and the members of the grassroots organizations in various parts of the country must demonstrate the universality of their faith and their serious commitment to break down all barriers that give rise to social and political movements for change in the country.

This volume is an important introduction of Islam and the Muslims in the United States of America to the members of the American reading public. The first essay, written by Dr. Asad Husain, provides the historical and sociological background to the present state of affairs among the Muslims. My foreward has amplified many of the themes and trends described in his essay. The second paper in this volume is an insightful analysis of the media coverage of Islam and the Muslims in American society. Written by a native-born American of European descent who has established a major reputation for himself among US students of the Muslim World and the Middle East, this second piece identifies the sources of the negative images of the American Muslims. Professor John Woods gives an effective mental guided tour of the damaged areas of Muslim social and psychological life in American society. His writing skills and his analytical mind have combined to shed light in areas where many Americans who unfamiliar with the Muslim record could easily be misled by the persistent and unrelenting denigrators of Muslims in the modern world. Woods' piece is an important addition to the collection and it is sandwiched between the historical/sociological analysis of Dr. Husain's and the policy oriented paper of Dr. Javeed Akhter, a member of this institute who has tried in his own way to communicate to Muslims and non-Muslims the frustrations of Americans of the Islamic faith when their fellow citizens allow past prejudices and stereotypes to determine how they relate to American Muslims. Like Dr. Martin Luther King of the American Civil Rights Movement, the good doctor would like his fellow citizens to judge him not by their prejudicial knowledge of Islam derived from hostile sources, but by the content of his character as a Muslim living faithfully his religion within the borders of the US. Indeed one can conclude here by saying that, according to Dr. Akhter, if men and women of conscience living in the US are able to shed the scales of prejudice inherited from the past and to engage in meaningful dialogue with their Muslim neighbors, chances are the old wounds of the Crusades would not be re-opened and America would be richer for it because the American Muslims are now strongly convinced that they have a message to their fellow Americans and a contribution to make towards the moral and material development of their homeland.

*Sulayman S. Nayang, Ph.D.*
*Howard University*

# A BRIEF HISTORY AND DEMOGRAPHICS OF MUSLIMS IN THE UNITED STATES

*Dr. Asad Husain*
*Imran Husain*

## INTRODUCTION

Perhaps only those who have watched Islam grow in the United States for over the last 60 years know the time of this religion to become well-recognized and respected is quietly, but surely approaching. The American Muslim is gradually merging into mainstream America, while striving to maintain his Islamic identity. However, the dramatic increase in Muslims have come at a time when the American public opinion is somewhat negative about Muslims, a result often fueled by inaccurate news provided by the media on Islam and Muslims.

Yet, interest in Islam has been increasing. Curious minds, scholars, professionals, lawyers, and even politicians are trying to learn about a religion which they perceive as very rigid and well disciplined in a society which values and promotes materialistic pursuits above all other human endeavors and wherein all luxury goods and amenities of life are accessible to the community. All that is prohibited in Islam is available quite easily to the people. In spite of these and other difficulties Muslims have established mosques, schools, foundations and other institutions. Like their Christian and Jewish counterparts, Muslims are attempting to find a niche in the society where a better life in the community is possible through the teachings and practices of their religion.

Yvonne Haddad writes, "the situation of Muslims in America must be understood in terms of dynamics of their relationship to their environment in the United States and its influence on the development of Islamic ideas throughout the modern world."[1] What the Muslim community in America faces are challenges that have not been encountered since the birth of Islam. Although it is in a land where it is still the minority, it is growing and acquiring new opportunities to expand. Over the years Muslim organizations and centers have provided a framework for Muslims to practice their religion; and while the generalization is that Muslims are discordant with Western society, it should be asserted that they have been successful in the last two hundred years of starting their own Muslim community in American society.

HISTORICAL BACKGROUND

Muslim and non-Muslim scholars are speculating, debating, and arguing about the presence of Muslims in the Americas long before Christopher Columbus disembarked on the new shores in 1492. But, how Islam and its followers first came to America, is still a question to be answered. These early visitors left no signs of their permanent settlement in this country, and can only be determined from preliminary records.

According to Clyde-Ahmad Winters, in his documented article, "Islam in Early North and South America," he states "[the first thing] we must understand is that ancient America was not isolated from the Old World, as many anthropologists and historians would have us to believe; in Mexico and parts of Central and South America, people from the Old and New Worlds mingled and exchanged ideas before Columbus got information on Americas from the Muslims in North and West Africa."[2] Winter further quotes Barbara Fordís article "Semites First in America," in which she writes, "evidence leading to the presence of Muslims in ancient Americas comes from a passage of sculptures, oral traditions, eyewitness reports, artifacts, and inscriptions."[3] In addition, he quotes many authors to prove his point that Muslims did reach the shores of the America almost 180 years before Columbus reached here. The following passage is an excerpt from Winters' papers:

......From evidence available, it seems that the Muslim navigators arrived in the New World from Africa and Spain. This is supported by the Arab coins found off the coast of South America dating back to 800 A.D. and discussed by C. Gordon in "Before Columbus." These coins lend validity to al-Masudis claim that Muslims of Cordoba reached the New World.[4]

Dr. M. Hamidullah in his article which is quoted by Winters, quotes al-Masudi who in "Maru adh-Dhahab," written in the year 956, said, "in the ocean (Atlantic) of and fog here are many curiosities which we have mentioned in detail in our Akbar al-Zaman, adventurers who penetrated on the risk of their lives, some returning safely, others perishing in the attempt. A certain inhabitant of Cordoba, Khashash by name, assembled a group of young men, his co-citizens, and went voyage on this ocean," and that " after a long time he returned with booty; every Spaniard knows this story."[5]

There is no doubt this voyage as well as other possible adventures to the ancient America did not affect the history of the New World, mainly due to their limited explorations under-taken mostly by the Spanish Muslims. The significant journeys to the New World seem to have been those undertaken by the Mandin of West Africa- journeys which later led to the so-called discovery of the New World by Columbus.

In another event which also happened before the discov-ery of America by Columbus, the Emperor of Mali, Mansa Abubakari Muhammad, is reported to have set sail in the direction of the New World. The story of his voyage was told to the Governor of Cairo, by Emperor Mansa Musa, and then was recorded by the Arab historian, al-Umari.[6]

Mansa Abubakari Muhammad, son of Qu, believed it was possible to reach the other side of the Atlantic Ocean; so he took 200 ships of men and another 200 laden with gold, water, and supplies. One ship returned and reported they had detected a river in the middle of the sea. All the ships, he said, had entered the current that rose from the West. Upon receiving this message in 1312 A.D., Muhammad equipped 1,000 vessels with men and another 1,000 with supplies; and after Muhammad turned his empire to Mansa Musa, he embarked with his fleet in the direction of the New World.

Many scholars still do not believe these explorers led by Mansa Abubakari Muhammad reached America. But the two voyages to America by explorer Thor Heyerdahl along with numerous examples discovered by Leo Weiner and published in the book, Africa and the Discovery of the America, some corroboration may be acknowledged that Muhammad indeed reached America in pre-Columbus times.

According to Ibn Khaldun, the famous Arab sociologist, the Mali Empire extended to the Atlantic Coast. The river Casamance, which fell in the territory under Mansa Abubakris control offered a great launching site for his proposed voyage across the Atlantic.[7] It also seems that Manding explorers under Abubakari's instructions explored many parts of the United States. This is evident from the appearance of mounds throughout the United States, especially in the vicinity of the Mississippi River, which they used for exploring America. Leo Weiner has tried to prove that Mandings traded with the American-Indians along the East Coast, all the way to Canada. In Arizona they left inscriptions which show the Manding explorers bringing numbers of elephants to America with them. Writings and pictographs found in a cave at Four Corners, Arizona, describe the characteristics of the desert by the following:

1. "Ga-gya, Kpa-ngbe-ka-go-ne" (The desert is hot. Birds are numerous white.....(ka)....and called (go).
2. "elephant-ga-ki-Bi-Kpa" (The elephants are sick and angry. At present sick elephants are considerable.)[8]

## ARRIVAL OF EARLY MUSLIMS

The first known Muslims who landed here were Spanish artisans and slaves from West Africa. According to Nadim Makidisi, the first Muslim came to North America with Marcos de Niza and Franciscan Friar, who were sent to explore Arizona.[9] Subsequently, in the 1840s the well known Hi Jolly (otherwise known as Al-Haj Ali), of early Arizona and California history, was brought to the United States by government experts who thought camels could be bred on the Arizona desert. Although the project failed, Hi Jolly, who accompanied the camels from Arabia, remained out in the Western terrain of America and prospered in California.[10]

Very little information about these early Muslim immigrants is available. Their existence is mostly ascertained by some government records and oral reports. Dr. M.A. Rauf writes in his paper, Islam and Islamic Institutions in the Americas:[10]

The House of Representative of South Carolina permitted in 1790, "Sundry Moors", subjects of the Emperor of Morocco" to be tried in court in accordance with prevailing law. About the same time we hear of a debate in the South concerning the right of worship to Catholics, Jews and Muslims. Much earlier, a man by the name of "Nasr-al-Din," said to be a prince who came from Egypt, lived in the area of New York during the 16th century." He further writes, "We also encounter the name of Ben Ali, a North African whose descendants fought on the Confederate side during the Civil War. Moreover, a body of stringent legislatures created by Spain relating to

23

Muslim infiltration in Spanish America implies early existence of Muslims who apparently fled the persecution at home and sought freedom of worship in the newly discovered land.[11]

All these traces and fragmentary research do indicate the existence of Muslims in America since the very early days. However, the records of these early explorations need to be studied carefully and discussed before any definite answer can be given. The Muslim slaves who came and lived mostly in the Southern part of America faced similar difficulties as other slaves who came from Africa. The Muslim slaves were detected by their adherence to such well known Islamic dietary practices as abstaining from eating pork and using alcoholic drinks. On occasions these early slaves were noted to utter such words as "Allah" and "Muhammad" (p.b.u.h.). They also secretly practiced Islamic prayers. Alex Haley's 1977 monumental work *Roots* touched upon some of these facts. His African ancestor, Kunta Kinti, was from a Muslim family of Juffars in West Africa. He was the son of a Muslim chief, Umru.[12] Kunta Kinti shows dedication to his Islamic African heritage and a true defiance to oppression which is characteristic of Muslims everywhere. However, it is rather impossible to ascertain the number of Muslims, either slaves or free slaves, who came to America in the early days. However it is certain very little attention was paid to these Muslim slaves by their masters concerning their religion or religious beliefs.

European colonialism had been dominant all over Asia and Africa for a period of more than three hundred years. Colonial powers were busy suppressing the religious beliefs of almost all people other than their own. Thus, the regime was a barrier for those who wished to travel or migrate for higher values. When this barrier started to crack under the pressure of nationalist and religious movements, only then did a few Muslims get the opportunity to come to America.

The 19th century is a period which has recorded evidence of the Muslims' arrival in this country. For example, the Palestinian Muslims had come to Chicago and other parts of the United States as early as 1880. According to Dr. Abdul Jalil Al-Tahir who, in his unpublished thesis gave reasons and evidence of the Arabs mass departure. Although he is not certain, he writes as follows: "The homeland was in the grip of the feudal system until the civil war between the Christian Syrians and the Muslim Palestinians which took place in 1860. The peasants were rapidly losing proprietorship in the soil and becoming serfs. Christian Syrians and Muslim Palestinians sought security elsewhere.[13]

In the later part of the 19th century there were great upheavals in Eastern Europe and in the Middle East. By contrast, the Civil War in America had ended and there was more stability in the United States. This, coupled with improved navigational traffic, encouraged Muslims to seek other opportunities in the New World. During the same period the Czars were persecuting Muslims not only in the neighboring countries, but also their own subjects within Imperial Russia. This also created a migration pressure and many Muslims found themselves forced to move to the United States.

By the turn of this century, the political climate of Europe was getting cloudier. Great Britain and France were leaders of the colonial group of countries. The domineering Ottoman Empire was in disarray which encouraged the Arabs to nurture the idea of nationalism, a force which became more powerful than the brotherhood of Islam. Thus, the beginning of the 20th century was the time when the Turkish Empire was neither an Islamic State in the true religious sense nor an Arab and Turkish nation. The political intrigues and economic jealousies triggered World War I between Germany, on one hand, and Great Britain and France on the other in 1914. The Turkish Empire chose to be on the German side. Hence, when Germany was defeated in 1918, the breakup of the Turkish Empire was imminent. This breakup of the Turkish Empire resulted in the migration of Arabic speaking people to the United States on Turkish passports.[14] Many of them settled down in the Great Plains area, with their principal center in Cedar Rapids, Iowa. In addition, there was Highland Park, Michigan and Michigan City, Indiana, and other places such as Toledo, Ohio, New York City, Detroit, and Chicago. A small group of these people consisting of 20 Syrian Muslim families settled in Ross, North Dakota, while some of their kin moved out to Kansas and Nebraska.

During World War II, the Muslim population increased as well as the growth of their organizations. Accordingly, by the end of the war, there had been two major changes in the world: the re-drawing of many national boundaries; and a communications revolution. Furthermore, the stress of identity plus the facility to travel and political industrial factors seemed to have triggered a new wave of migration too.

The rise of militant communism, first in Russia and Central Asia and later Communist supremacy of Eastern Europe can be seen as the most important single factor in the migration of a large number of Muslims to the United States in the present century. Among the Muslims who migrated to America during this period were primarily those from the Soviet Union, Eastern Europe, Albania and Syria. Others that migrated during this period were Muslims from Africa, the Middle East and Asia who were serving or had served either in the colonial army or merchant navy.

Thus, the effect of World War II could be summarized as follows:
- The colonial period came to an end.
- Communism emerged as a threat to the new world.
- Development of atomic weapons introduced a new dimension to national power.
- Western Europe was no longer considered the seat of world power.
- The technological revolution had taken place which

brought the world closer.
• The economic order of the world was disrupted.
• Political balance in the world had changed.

## RECENT ARRIVAL OF MUSLIMS

Under various scholarships and United States programs, students came into almost all the major centers and universities of this new world. This influence also brought thousands of non-Muslim students from different parts of the world. Among those who first arrived were the ones who had suffered repression in Eastern European countries, followed by people from the Indian sub-continent, who came after the partition of India in 1947, and the police action by India in the Hyderabad State in 1948. Similarly, the establishment of Israel in 1948 injected political instability, ideological confusion, and internal conflict into the Middle East, which forced thousands of Muslims to immigrate to America from the Arab world. Other cases were the separation of Bangladesh from Pakistan in 1971-1972, and the civil war in Lebanon which caused even more Muslims to seek refuge in the United States. Still, Muslim immigrants came to the United States for many reasons, some of which were for economic and political security.[15]

## THE FOUR WAVES OF IMMIGRATION

Often immigration happens in waves, with droves of new-comers arriving in large numbers to a new country after they have received news from family or acquaintances who have recently settled in the new land. Muslim immigrants have been no exception. Haddad writes of four waves of Muslim immi-grants, with the first coming just before World War I composed of primarily Muslims departing from the collapsed Ottoman Empire.[16] Yet, during this time and even before there were not many indigenous people in America who accepted the religion of

Islam in America. The few who did were considered to be intellectuals. The earliest known American to embrace the faith was Alexander Russell Webb.[17] In 1887, he was sent to the Philippines at Manila as the American Consul where he came into contact with local and Indian Muslims and was influenced by the teachings of Islam. In 1888, he wrote a pamphlet in which he stated, "Islam is founded upon the eternal truth which has been handed to man from age to age, by chosen prophets of God; it is the only system known to man which is strictly in harmony with reason and science." He further wrote, "I adopted this religion because I found, after protracted study, that it was the best and only system adapted to the spiritual needs of humanity."[18]

The second wave also came from mainly the Middle East and settled in the Midwest, looking for blue-collar labor. One location which has become well known for its massive Arab population as well as its Islamic organizations is Dearborn, Michigan. Ever since the 1920s when the first few Arabs arrived, the community has emerged as a prominent force in the Dearborn vicinity. During the late 1930s and early 1940s it was even considered to be the largest and most powerful voting block in the town. In fact, in an interview conducted by Wigle, "90 percent of the first generation Arabs reported they had lineage ties with other residents in the South End district of Dearborn prior to their arrival in America, many of whom were Muslims."[19]

The third wave was after World War II to the mid-1960s. With the division of Arabia into smaller states and the establishment of Israel, many Muslims fled from political oppression. From all over the Middle East, Palestinian refugees and Muslims fleeing from political revolution swings in the nations of Egypt, Jordan, and Syria immigrated to the United States. However, many of these Muslims possessed wealth and academic merit which led them to find white-collar occupations in big cities and metropolitan areas.

The fourth wave was ignited during the pinnacle of the Vietnam War. At this time President Lyndon Johnson's Great

Society plan encouraged a more progressive and diverse America that gave relatively easy access for immigration. This spurred an entire new generation of foreign Muslims to enter America. This wave comprised largely of Muslims from the Indo-Pak-Bangladesh subcontinent. In addition, Muslim countries sent students to America to learn western education and technology which could help the progress of their own countries. The developing oil countries also sent thousands of young men to America to gain skills and education needed for technological development.

DEMOGRAPHICS

Although there is no figure which is currently up to date on the population of Muslims in the United States, the figure is estimated at six million. Currently, Islam is believed to be the fastest growing religion in America. This entails several ethnic populations comprised of a significant percentage of Muslims who lived in America as well as trends in immigration to America.

The number of Muslim immigrants living in the United States has been statistically evaluated from three sets of data: (1) A 1990 census statistic of the countries from which immigrants came to the United States; (2) the country of ancestry from which immigrants came; and (3) the number of Muslims from Muslim countries.

Although the 1990 U.S. Statistical Abstract did not mention the number of Muslims, figures were extrapolated using 1990 immigration census statistics, American Muslims Council statistics and Stone's 1980 statistical evaluation on the number of Muslims. The number of Muslims living in the United States in 1990 was assessed between 5 and 6 million. These figures were also estimated by leading American newspapers. This estimate represented 1.9 to 2.2 percent of the total 264,000,000 U.S. population. Table 1 lists a breakdown of the Muslim ancestry and their numbers who now live in the United States.[20] These data indicate that it is not the Muslims from the Middle East and South Asia, but converted African-Americans who constitute the largest group of Muslims in America.

African-Americans constituted approximately 30 millions people of the U.S. population in 1996 with 8.0 percent of them being Muslims. This comprises for 42 percent of the U.S. Muslim population. The next largest group (24.4%) is Muslims from South Asia (India, Pakistan , Bangladesh, Sri Lanka and Afghanistan). The Arabs constitute 12.4% of the Muslim American population. (Table 1)[21]

In 1986 the Muslim population in America was estimated at four million. This indicates an increase of 21 percent over the six-year period from 1980 to 1986. With the assumption that this increase will remain constant, by the year 2000, this population may increase to approximately 10 to 12 millions.

REGIONAL CONCENTRATION

In a 1990 census statistics regional concentrations were surveyed for the concentrations of Muslims living in America. Of the fifty states, three were selected for study: Illinois, California, and New York. The results of the study showed California with the highest Muslim population with 600,000, followed by New York with 500,000 and Illinois with 350,000 (Table 2). Hence, approximately half of the Muslim population in America is concentrated in these three states. Moreover, California contained the largest number of Middle East and African Muslims in the country, New York had the largest number of African-American Muslims, while Illinois equally represented the Muslim ancestries listed in Table 1.[22]

One note should be worth mentioning. Although California contains the largest population of Middle East and African immigrants, the town of Dearborn, Michigan has the highest concentration of Arabs outside the Middle East. Almost

70,000 Arabs live in a concentrated area just outside of the Detroit area. However, there are unofficial reports that this statistic may even be higher.[23]

MUSLIM IMMIGRATION AND POPULATION

In the last two decades the number of Muslim immigrants has doubled, increasing from four percent of all immigrants in 1968 to 10.5 percent. Muslim immigration can be divided among the following subdivisions of countries: Asia, the Middle East, Africa, Turkey, Iran, Afghanistan and Bosnia.[24]

The overall Muslim immigrant population showed a steady increase between 1971-1990 (Table 3). However, after 1990 the immigrant population to the United States from these countries has declined. One reason has been the present United States regulations on the allotment of immigrants that are allowed to enter each year. The 1995 Immigration Bill has reduced the number of visas being issued each year, which has resulted in fewer Muslim immigrants.

For example, in a 1993 count, the number of Syrian immigrants declined  from 13,300 per year entering the United States between 1971-1980, to 2,900. Turkey which brought a hefty 20,900 per year between 1981-1990, reduced to a mere 2,200, an 88 percent reduction. Other countries have had a similar trend over the last twenty five years, as shown in Table 3, U.S. Abstract on Statistical Figures, 1995.[25]

It is known that at the time of the 1980 Iranian revolution, there were almost 500,000 Iranian, Malaysians and Arab students. Likewise, these students at their respective universities have built mosques and organizations which has led to an attraction for new immigrants to come to America.[26]

EMERGENCE OF MUSLIM ORGANIZATIONS

From the influx of Muslim students from different political and religious backgrounds, to the campuses of higher learning in the United States, the emergence of a national Islamic organization came to the forefront of the Muslims' commitment to preserve Islam in the United States. One of the first Islamic organizations was established in New York City in 1938 known as the Moorish National Islamic Center. Later, a much larger group, the International Muslim Society, was also founded in New York as well as the Islamic Mission of America was formed in Brooklyn. Other organizations and were later established in such cities as Detroit, Chicago, Washington, D.C., and Philadelphia.

As a result of the of increasing numbers of Muslims every year in the United States, the acquisitions of buildings went underway to develop mosques. Historically, Muslim scholars speculate the first mosque was the Mother Mosque of Cedar Rapids, known as Umma al-Masjid Fi Amerikia, built in 1925. However, according to Dr. Abdo El-Kholy, the first mosque was built in Highland Park, Michigan in 1919, with perhaps the second one founded in Michigan City, Indiana in 1924.[27] Regardless which institution was established first, these places of worship gradually increased promoting Islamic centers throughout the country. Currently, there are nearly 2000 mosques in the United States.

In the initial stages the activities of many of these organizations were generally confined to social, religious, and cultural activities; but eventually they merged to form a National Muslim Students' Association with more comprehensive aims and objectives. By 1960, most major universities had some kind of Muslim student's society or association which led to the establishment of the Muslim Student Association of the United States and Canada on January 1, 1963, at the University of Illinois in Urbana. These organizations received a measure of support both from their respective colleges and the local communities. The MSA is considered to be the most active among the Muslim organizations at a national level, with chapters at nearly 200 campuses. The MSAs held conferences annually which attracted a number of

Muslim students and non-Muslim students.

At the community level there exists an organization known as the Federation of Islamic Associations (FIA). The idea to form an FIA was first conceived at a gathering in Cedar Rapids, Iowa in 1952, and later established in 1954 in Chicago. However, the Federation has not been able to satisfy the needs of the Muslim community on a national level. The idea of having an Islamic Center in Washington, D.C. became a reality with the help of the Muslim countries of the world in 1949, which was formally opened in 1957. Although essentially a local body, this center carries great prestige and is a focus of many Muslim activities in the country. Similarly, the Islamic Cultural Center of New York, located in downtown Manhattan is a functional place for the Muslim activities. This center is run and controlled by the Muslim Ambassadors to the United Nations.

But perhaps the most well-recognized Islamic organization to help Muslim students and citizens is the Islamic Society of North America (ISNA). Founded in 1982 with its headquarters in Plainsfield, Indiana, ISNA sponsors activities throughout the country including their annual convention that currently attracts about 10,000 to 15,000 Muslims every year. Similarly, the Islamic Circle of North America (ICNA) holds annual conventions as well as conferences that bring a great number of Muslims to their events.

There are also several other Muslim organizations. The American Muslim Council (AMC) was formed in June of 1990 with the intention of providing aid to American-Muslim communities and tries to promote Islam as an active participant in the American legal system and socio-political activities. In fact, the AMC set up a legal department in 1992 to handle cases concerning issues such as child custody, religious rights and hate crimes against Muslims.[28]

Professional groups such as the Islamic Medical Association, Association of Muslim Social Scientists, Association of Muslim Scientists and Engineers, Council of American

Muslim Professionals (CAMP), and the North American Association of Muslim Professionals and Scholars (NAAMPS) are quite prominent in America. Although their activities vary due to diverse occupations, they more or less are of the same nature.

MUSLIM PARTICIPATION IN AMERICAN
POLITICAL SYSTEM

Muslim organizations have not stopped with limited plans to preserve their identity and religion through schools and community centers. Recently, Muslims are increasingly getting involved in the political spectrum. They have supported candidates from both major parties. However, their voting strength was first noted in Chicago when Harold Washington was elected as the first Afro-American mayor with bloc support from the Muslims of Chicago. The League of Muslim voters played an important role in this 1983 Mayoral election. Since then they have participated in the Democratic and Republican conventions of 1984, 1988, 1992 and 1996. In the 1994 election Muslim groups backed 77 congressional and gubernatorial candidates. This year the American Muslim Alliance and other Muslim political organizations are mounting an effort to support a presidential candidate based on policies beneficial to both American and Muslim interests. Although Muslims constitute only 2.2% of the total U.S. population, they are concentrated in states with large numbers of electoral votes (California, New York, Ohio, Michigan, and Illinois). This offers them a strategic advantage in a presidential election.

Muslims have also been active in the following events:
- Muslims have been very active in school council elections in most cities where many of them have been elected.
- On the national level they fostered Muslims candidates for congressional positions from Los Angeles, San

34

Francisco, and Chicago.
- 50,000 Muslims from all over the country gathered in Washington, D.C. on May 13, 1993 to show their concern and support for Bosnian Muslims during the height of Yugoslavia's civil war.
- In 1995 Muslims also demonstrated in front of the United Nations building in New York as well as other cities to show their support for Bosnian Muslims.

Some of the organizations that are currently politically active are: the Muslim Political Action Committee (MPAC); Council of American Islamic Relations (CAIR); the League of Muslim Voters; and the American Muslim Alliance.

## ACTIVITIES AND CONFERENCES

Muslim Organizations such as ISNA (Islamic Society Of North America), ICNA (Islamic Circle Of North America ), NAAMPS (North American Association of Muslim Professionals and Scientists) and CAMP (Council Of American Muslim Professionals) hold conferences every year. Currently, there have been attempts to coordinate a Muslim lobby aimed at influencing the 1996 Presidential elections. Likewise, the most recognized Muslim associations have come together to form the Fiqh Council which serves to guide the community by giving interpretation on various Islamic issues that are referred to it.

Recently, another organization has emerged as an important force in the world that has not only affected Muslims but the followers of other religions as well. The Parliament of the World's Religions; an organization that promotes inter-faith harmony among all religions and strives for global peace, had its very first gathering in 1893 at Chicago. At that time only one American Muslim represented Islam. One hundred years later, the Parliament commemorated its 100th anniversary at the very same location in a week long festivity that included lectures, seminars, panels and exhibits. Among them 500 Muslim delegates from around the world attended the event marking the first time an extraordinary opportunity was provided for fostering fellowship and camaraderie among various religious communities. Thus, an Islamic Host Group in the United States was established in order to represent Islam and to improve relations among communities of different religions. The Islamic Host Group continues to endeavor toward its goal of providing a better understanding of Islam and Muslims in the United States and in the world.[29]

FAMOUS MUSLIMS IN AMERICA

Fazlur Rahman, a structural engineer from Bangladesh, gained world renown in 1970 by designing the well-known Sears Tower and John Hancock buildings which now grace the Chicago skyline. Scholars of Islamic studies such as Professor Fazlur Rahman of the University of Chicago, Professor Ismail al-Faruqi of Temple University, and Syed Hossein Nasr of George Washington University have made invaluable contribution towards a better understanding of Islam in the United States. And of course, the honorable Malcom X (Malik Shabbaz), whose monumental contributions to the African-American and Islamic communities are still felt to this day.

Muslims have contributed immensely to the American society in many professions, particularly in the field of Medicine, Engineering, Architecture and many other scientific disciplines. They have been equally successful as entrepreneurs. Safi Qureshi , the CEO and the founder of AST Computers in California; a well known figure in the Silicone Valley, is a notable example.

There have also been sports figures like Kareem Abdul Jabbar, one of the greatest basketball players ever to set foot on the court, surprised many when he converted to Islam and went on to win 6 National Basketball Association championships in his career along with the most points ever scored by any one individual. Muhammad Ali, perhaps the greatest boxer and athlete of the last century, defeated all challengers who tried to dethrone him. There are still others: Hakeem Olijuwan, 2-time NBA champion; Mahmoud Abdul-Rauf, all-star basketball guard; Eddie Murray, first baseman for the Baltimore Orioles and soon-to-be Hall of Famer; and Mike Tyson, heavyweight boxing champion considered by many to be the best in the boxing today.

THE FOCUS FOR TOMORROW

In the coming years one major focus for Muslims is to establish clear and cordial communications with the other American communities. With ever increasing alternatives available to communicate, namely new emerging "technologies", "information super highway", Muslims must take advantage of these options and establish their own credible communication outlets. That is the only way they can dispel misunderstanding and misinformation about Islam and Muslims.

Another focus for Muslims should be to foster strong unity and brotherhood among themselves by overcoming the ethnic divides. Recently the Afro-American Muslims who constitute 40% of all Muslims in America, have been a source of strength to all Muslims.

Although there is still debate on how to effect synthesis of Islam and the West, Muslims have shown strong signs of making progress in this direction. This clearly is a harbinger of happy times for the next generation American Muslims and beyond.

# Table 1

## ETHNIC DISTRIBUTION

### Muslims in America (1992)

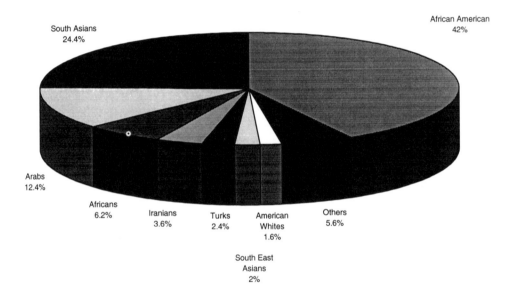

South Asians
24.4%

African American
42%

Arabs
12.4%

Africans
6.2%

Iranians
3.6%

Turks
2.4%

American
Whites
1.6%

Others
5.6%

South East
Asians
2%

Table 2

Total Muslim Population Spread in US Cities

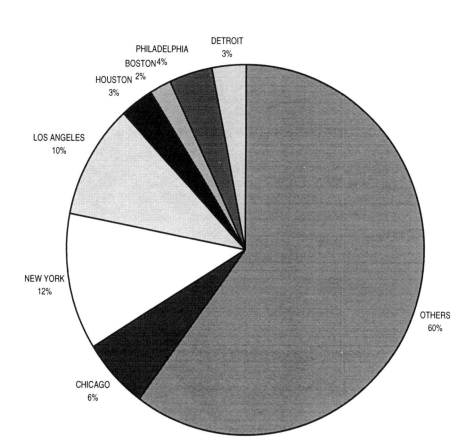

# Table 3

## Muslim Immigration to the United States from 1971 to 1993

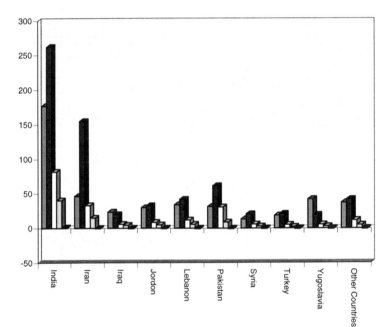

| Countries | 1971-1980 | 1981-1990 | 1991-1992 | 1993 | Change |
|---|---|---|---|---|---|
| India | 176.8 | 261.9 | 81.8 | 40.1 | 77% |
| Iran | 46.2 | 154.8 | 32.8 | 14.8 | -67% |
| Iraq | 23.4 | 19.6 | 5.6 | 4.1 | -82% |
| Jordon | 29.6 | 32.6 | 8.3 | 4.7 | -84% |
| Lebanon | 33.8 | 41.6 | 11.8 | 5.5 | -83% |
| Pakistan | 31.2 | 61.3 | 30.6 | 8.9 | -71% |
| Syria | 13.3 | 20.6 | 5.8 | 2.9 | -78% |
| Turkey | 18.6 | 20.9 | 5 | 2.2 | -88% |
| Yugoslavia | 42.1 | 19.2 | 5.3 | 2.8 | -93% |
| Other Cou | 37.3 | 41.9 | 11.5 | 4.9 | -87% |

[1] Yvonne Haddad, *Muslims of America*, Oxford University Press, New York, 1987, pp. 180-200.

[2] Clyde-Ahmad Winters, "Islam in Early North and South America," July-October, 1977, p.57, *Al-Ittihad*.

[3] Ibid, p.57.

[4] Ibid, p.57.

[5] Ibid, p.58.

[6] Ibid, p.59.

[7] Ibid. p.60-61.

[8] Nadim Makdisi, "The Muslims in America," *The Christian Century*, 1959, p.969.

[9] Emily Kalled Lowell, "A Survey of the Arab-Muslims in the United States and Canada," April, 1973, p.143, *The Muslim World*.

[10] M.A. Rauf, "Islam and Islamic Institutions in North America," Vol. 6-77, April, 1976, p.43, *Impact*.

[11] Alex Haley, *Roots*, Doubleday Press, New York, 1976.

[12] Ibid, p.97.

[13] Abdul-Jalil al-Tahir, The Community in the Chicago Area: A Comparative Study of the Christian Syrians and the Muslim Palestinians, unpublished, University of Chicago, 1977.

[14] Ibid, p.75.

[15] Warner and Srole describe in their study of ethnic groups, "forces of attraction" as an act exerted by expanding American economy, and "forces of expulsion" exerted in the lands of immigrants Lloyd W. Warner and Leo Srole, *The Social System of American Ethnic Groups*, New Haven, Yale University, 1945, p.105.

[16] Yvonne Haddad, op.cit., pp. 180-200.

[17] M.A. Rauf, op.cit., p.44.

[18] Ibid, p.68.

[19] Imran Husain, "Dearborn Muslim Community: A Culture Within A Culture," April 1996, *The Minaret*, p.19-23.

[20] Fareed H Nu'man, "The Muslim Population in the United States", p.16, The American Muslim Council, December 1992.

[21] Ibid, p.16.

[22] Ibid, p.16; Asad Husain, Harold Volegar, "Activities of the Immigrant Muslim Communities in Chicago," Yvonne Haddad and Jane Smith, *Muslim Communities in North America*, State University of New York Press, 1985, 231-259.

[23] Imran Husain, op.cit. p.21.

[24] The influx of Muslims from Afghanistan and Bosnia were due to the brutal attacks that each of the respective governments had faced. Afghanistan was suppressed by the former Soviet Union; Bosnia, by Serbia.

[25] U.S. Abstract on Statistical Figures, 1995. Note: The number was estimated by taking the number of immigrants who arrive

each year from predominantly Muslim countries; taking the actual percentage of Muslims from the total population of those counties and calculating the number of Muslim immigrants from the total immigrant population that came to the United States. The inferential statistic is addressed to sampling errors and do not account for nonsampling errors.

[26] Yvonne Haddad, *Islamic Communities in North America*, New York Press, New York, 1994, p.xxii-xxiii.

[27] Asad Husain "Muslims in America," manuscript, 1995, p.-58.

[28] George Braswell, *Islam: Its Prophet, Peoples, Politics, and Power*, Broadman & Holdman, p.212.

[29] Imran Husain, "Muslims Participate in the Parliament of Worlds Religions," July/August 1993, p.25-27, *The Minaret*.

# IMAGINING AND STEREOTYPING ISLAM

*John E. Woods*
*The University of Chicago*

...And now what will become of us without barbarians?
Those people were a kind of solution.[1]

Over the last decade, I have had the opportunity to speak to a number of audiences throughout the United States about aspects of Islamic history and civilization. Before beginning each presentation, I attempted to assess the knowledge and attitude of the group by distributing a sheet with the following instructions:

Imagine you are a pollster standing in a shopping mall (school quadrangle, etc.) stopping passersby and asking the question, What concepts, nouns, and adjectives come to mind when you hear the words "Muslim," "Islam," "Arab," or "Middle East?" Please list below what you think their responses might be.

After five minutes or so, I would ask the audience to call out some of the words they had listed and I would write them on the blackboard: "barbaric, treacherous, land grabbers, freaks, vengeful, sand nigger, corrupt, irrational, heretics, smelly" are typical examples of their reactions. Collecting and tabulating almost 5,000 of these sheets, I was astounded to see that virtually all the words listed there were negative and insulting; almost never was a positive attribute or quality mentioned. As an educator, I was concerned that if such notions were held by my audiences, they would be likely to produce denial and rejection of any new information that I might provide rather than facilitate the acceptance and internalization of new learning that is sometimes called paradigm shift. As Walter Lippmann wrote, "The only feeling that anyone can have about an event he does not experience is the feeling aroused by his mental image of that event." He then emphasized the necessity to know "what others think they know" in order to understand their actions and to establish the basis for a common understanding with them.[2] I therefore resolved to try to discover more about the origin and nature of such attitudes, why people hold them, and how they could be combated. This essay describes my explorations.

In the early 1990s, a series of public opinion research projects conducted by three national organizations made it abundantly clear that, in addition to those people who had attended my lectures, other segments of the American population harbored strong negative stereotypes of the Middle East and the Islamic World. In 1991, for example, the American Jewish Committee commissioned a study of contemporary American attitudes toward Jews.[3] As a part of the research design, survey respondents were requested to consider the following: "America is land made up of many different kinds of people. Some of these people have a higher social standing than others do... They were then asked to classify 58 ethnic, national, and religious groups from highest to lowest according to their social standing. Included as a control among these groups was a fictitious ethnicity, the Wisians. The results showed Gypsies lowest on the scale at number 58 with Iranians at 57 and Arabs at 47; both Middle Eastern groups ranked lower than the Wisians who were 45th.

Jews, incidentally, were number 20 after Danes, French Canadians, and Japanese.

The American Muslim Council and the Zogby Group carried out a similar, but less complex survey of American attitudes toward Muslims after the World Trade Center bombing in February 1993.[4] Out of almost 1,000 adults surveyed, 36% viewed Muslims unfavorably while only 23% viewed them favorably. The remaining 41% had no opinion. 43% of the respondents agreed with the statement that Muslims "tend to be religious fanatics" and nearly one-third concurred that "Muslims are not tolerant of others." Although the pollsters took some solace in the fact that 42% of those canvassed believed that there was a tendency to discriminate against Muslims, 20% thought that "Muslim population in the United States is growing too rapidly."

Finally, in 1994, The National Conference formerly known as The National Conference of Christians and Jews published the results of a nationwide survey of the opinions of nearly 3,000 Americans of different backgrounds on inter-group relations.[5] While the poll confirmed the persistence of prejudice by white groups toward minorities, it also demonstrated that minority groups also held negative images of other minority groups. Most of the non-Muslim groups surveyed Latino Americans, Whites, African Americans, and Asian Americans were relatively unified in their beliefs, however, that Muslims belong to a religion that condones or supports terrorism (40%), that they are anti-Western and anti-American (47%), and that they segregate and suppress women (62%). On the other hand, the survey reported that from 70% to 85% of the non-Muslim respondents thought that Muslims were deeply religious people who followed a strict code of personal behavior, who took pride in their cultural and religious heritage, and who were strongly committed to the welfare of their own people and communities. It should be noted that these positive stereotypes so called in the report could also be (and frequently are) construed as portraying Muslims in

47

America as inward-looking and isolationist. The National Conference interpretation, though doubtless well-intentioned, leaves an impression that is ambivalent at best.

Similar is the affect of this editorial cartoon published just after the World Trade Center bombing. First of all, the phrase "The only good Muslim..." echoes the expression "The only good Injun is a dead Injun." Furthermore, its condescending nature is immediately revealed when the word "Muslim" is replaced by the name of the follower of any other religion.

Given the nature of the views expressed in these surveys, it is not surprising that there occurred an immediate outpouring of anti-Muslim, anti-Middle Eastern feeling here and abroad as news of the tragic bombing in Oklahoma City spread. This backlash was triggered by irresponsible media commentators and government agencies who linked the attack to Arabs, Muslims, and Middle Easterners. "Terrorism expert" Steven Emerson stated on the CBS Evening News, for example, "this (the bombing) was done with the intent to inflict as many casualties as possible. That is a Middle Eastern trait;" the Oklahoma City police issued orders for the arrest of "three men with Middle Eastern appearance" whatever that may mean. Attitudes were subsequently translated into actions and the Council on American-Islamic Relations documented more than 220 instances of threats, assaults, harassments, and other hate crimes against Muslims and Middle Easterners in the days immediately following the tragedy as compared with 119 such crimes in all of 1991, the year of the Gulf War.[6]

Like the word "cliche", "stereotype" is a term originally derived from printing. It was given its current sense in the 1920s by Walter Lippmann in his work *Public Opinion* mentioned above. He used the term generally to refer to a way of perception that today might also include notions like "conceptual framework," "paradigm," or "working model." For him, however, it also specifically denoted a distorted picture or image in a persons mind, not based on personal experience, but derived culturally. In other words, he saw it as a form of inadequate deduction that involves defining a thing before it is experienced. Lippmann further pointed out that for political or economic motives or for convenience whole societies develop stereotypes, that these stereotypes are shared and passed on from generation to generation, and that they are resistant to change and thus very long-lived. Finally, he believed that stereotypes could be manipulated by a person or group to influence the way others feel, think, and act a process he termed "the manufacture of consent."[7]

For governments and other organizations, Lippmann's "manufacture of consent" has an obvious pragmatic use, namely the alignment of citizens or individuals behind official policy. It is especially important in times of war when governments find it necessary to override the ethical sanctions found in most religious systems against the taking of human life. In this case, stereotyping acquires the particular function of "enemy making," that is, the construction by the protagonist (us or the "in-group")

 of the antagonist (them, the "out-group," or the "Other") in such a way that it ultimately legitimizes killing members of the out-group by the in-group. It is therefore clear that stereotyping or construction of the Other also provides a standard or foil against which the in-group defines itself through a series of polar oppositions: "We are truthful, they are liars, We are rational, they are irrational," etc.

Two other uses of stereotypes should also be noted. The first is psychological and the second epistemological. Closely related to the preceding point, the first is that in constructing a foil, we thereby designate a scapegoat onto which we can project those negative qualities in ourselves that we find unacceptable and intolerable. This in turn suggests that this process is deep-seated in the human psyche and is perhaps essential to it. In connection to our knowledge of the world around us, stereotyping also helps reduce the threat of the unknown by making that world simple and predictable. Lippmann aptly characterizes all three usages in the following passage:

> ...The systems of stereotypes may be the core of our personal tradition, the defenses of our position in society. They may not be a complete picture of the world, but they are a picture of a possible world to which we are adapted. In that world people and things have their well-known places, and do certain expected things. We feel at home there. No wonder, then, that any disturbance of the stereotypes seems like an attack upon the foundations of the universe. [The pattern of stereotypes] is the projection upon the world of our own sense of our own value, our own positions and our own rights. The stereotypes are, therefore, highly charged with the feelings that are attached to them. They are the fortress of our tradition,

and behind its defenses we can continue to feel ourselves safe in the positions we occupy.[8]

Structurally, stereotyping takes the form of a "vicious regression." Rooted in ignorance, misconceptions, and negative images or attitudes, the stereotype provides a distorted mental picture or set of images which develop through reductionism into prejudice, bias, and eventually racism. This descent from ignorance into prejudice, bias, and racism can cause a person irrationally to exclude other individuals, that is, to discriminate against them.

The process of reductionism deserves closer scrutiny since it involves two powerful, related rhetorical tropes, synecdoche and metonymy, a discussion of which is relevant to our topic. Synecdoche is a figure of speech - and a mode of thought - in which a part of something is taken to represent the whole, the specific to represent the general or vice versa, or the material to represent the thing from which it is composed. Examples are *hand* for *sailor*, *law* for *policeman*, or *steel* for *sword*. Metonymy consists of substituting a word, phrase, or concept for another with which it is closely associated as in the use of *Washington* for the *United States government*. Understanding both is essential to our task since they are operative in the fabrication of stereotypes of Islam and Muslims. In the first place, any individual Muslim can stand for all Muslims or the government of any Muslim state for the governments of all Muslim states. Moreover, no differentiation is made between an Arab and a Muslim or between a Moroccan and an Indonesian. In the second, objects associated in the popular imagination with the Middle East - the area in which Islam, Judaism, and Christianity arose - such as camels, flowing robes, tents, and sand come to denote metonymically the entirety of Islamic religion and civilization. Similarly, Saddam Hussein represents all Iraqis and Khomeini all Iranians - both or either can stand for all Muslims as in the rogues gallery below. Finally, Islamic religion and culture are seen as monolithic - there is no distinction between religious and secular, between sacred and profane.

Western misconceptions, negative images, and stereotypes of the Islamic World have a long history and are deeply rooted in European political culture. For over a millennium, the Islamic World was Europe's most significant Other, representing an alien rival ideological, political, economic, and social system. In the West, the religion of Islam was seen as an outlandish heresy propagated through violence by the savage followers of an epileptic impostor. Barbaric Muslim powers successfully challenged European political and economic interests first in the

Mediterranean basin and later in Southern Europe and elsewhere. Finally, women in the Islamic World and their alleged position in Muslim society aroused both the prurient fascination and the moral indignation of European observers. Conflict in all these areas created a repertory of tropes that Europeans employed for centuries in framing the Muslim Other.[9] As the balance of power shifted in favor of Western Europe in the 18th and 19th centuries, these same negative constructs were then used to justify the conquest and subjugation of vast areas of the Islamic World. Colonial France "Civilizing Mission" and Britain's "White Man's Burden" were undergirded by notions directly derived from the medieval concepts discussed above.[10]

As a cultural extension of Western Europe, the United States initially inherited many of these images and ideas, but until relatively recently lacked a suitable context in which to place them. With the sole exception of the war against the Barbary pirates of North Africa at the beginning of the 19th century, neither the American government nor the American people had had much actual experience or contact with the Islamic World. In World War I, moreover, the United States did not declare war on the Ottoman Empire, even though President Wilson believed an equitable post-war settlement in the Middle East was in the American national interest. This situation changed radically at end of World War II when the United States as a new world power found itself heir to many of the political problems of European colonialism as well.

In the last 50 years, political, religious, social, and economic factors have had a great impact on the way Americans view the Middle East and the Islamic World. In a very short span of time from 1946 to 1953, for example, the foundations of the major issues in American foreign relations with the Islamic World were laid. First and foremost was the threat of the Cold War and the spread of Soviet Communism in the Middle East. First, in 1946, the fledgling United Nations Organization was faced with the challenge of Soviet reluctance to withdraw from

Iran and the creation of short-lived Soviet republics in Iranian Azarbayjan and Kurdistan. The stage was thus set for a series of encounters between the US and the USSR through their proxies in the Middle East over the next half century. Secondly, the creation of the state of Israel in 1948 along with the consequent dispossession of a large part of the Palestinian population and the hostility of the surrounding Arab states also created great instability in the region and has become a source of major concern for the US government and a sizable segment of the American people. The disruption and bitterness engendered by these developments have spread far beyond the Middle East and continue to imperil peace today. Third was the rise of anti-colonial forms of nationalism and the danger they posed to colonial and neo-colonial economic interests. CIA complicity in the overthrow of the government of Iranian premier Muhammad Musaddiq (Mossadegh) in 1953 over the nationalization of the Iranian petroleum industry marks the first direct US involvement in the affairs of a Middle Eastern state for this reason. This intervention was often invoked as a rallying point by anti-American groups during the upheavals in that country in 1978 and 1979.

But it was during the 1970s that most Americans began to feel themselves directly affected by events in the Middle East and the Islamic World. The Arab oil boycott in retaliation for US support of Israel in the 1973 Middle East war hit Americans economically at home, producing increased fuel costs, long lines at service stations, and a federally-imposed 55 mile-per-hour speed limit. In 1979 and 1980, the spectacle of American hostages held in Iran for more than a year was regular fare on the evening news and the failure of the US government to effect their release eventually brought down the Carter presidency. In the early 1980s, a number of Americans lost their lives in the Middle East, the greatest tragedy occurring in 1983 in Beirut when a US military base was attacked resulting in 241 fatalities. Middle Eastern-related bombings, hijackings, hostage takings, and assassinations abroad seemed almost a daily occurrence and

Americans were frustrated with the impotence of their government to prevent them. Some of these feelings were dispelled in 1986 when Ronald Reagan ordered the bombing of Libya to avenge an attack on a German discothèque frequented by US service men. This vindication, however, paled in comparison with that generated in the wake of the Gulf War which was seen not only as a triumph in itself of the forces of good over evil, but also as a final laying to rest of the specter of defeat in Viet Nam. This euphoria swiftly dissipated in 1993, however, when Americans were deeply traumatized by the bombing of the World Trade Center in New York carried out by a small group of Muslim religious fanatics - the battle was now being waged on the territory of the United States.

With the cultural background and the recent historical context of American attitudes toward the region, it seems natural that after the dissolution of the Soviet Union in 1991 the Islamic World was now immediately cast in the role of the "Evil Empire," as the USSR had been dubbed by Ronald Reagan in a 1983 speech to the National Association of Evangelists. In fact, it had been suggested as early as 1957 that Islam was one of only three ideologies competing for peoples allegiance in the modern world, the other two being Communism and Western liberal capitalism.[11] Russian Communism now defunct, the field was cleared for the two remaining contenders to struggle for supremacy in the post-Cold War world. A new external Other - the Green Wave of Islam - had arisen to replace the old antagonists the Red Menace and the Yellow Peril. The scenario of a possible future collusion of Chinese  Communism with Islam recently projected by Samuel Huntington, a prestigious Harvard professor of political science, thus rolls all three threats into a single multi-colored mega-enemy.[12]

In connection with Reagan's statement mentioned above, it is additionally important to note that Islam plays a significant if negative role in the views of evangelical or fundamentalist-dispensationalist Christians, many of whom believe that the end of the world will take place in the relatively near future. Among the signs of this cataclysm foretold in the Bible is the reestablishment of Israel, the return of Jerusalem to Jewish control, the rise of a new Roman Empire in the form of the EEC, and the attack on Israel by Russians, East Europeans, Arabs, and Africans. The enthusiastic evangelical championing of the Israeli government and its policies is sometimes called Christian Zionism, the obverse of which is an equally fervent hostility to Islam. Moreover, anti-Communism, which also figured centrally in evangelical Christianity, has been redirected towards Islam since 1991. For the evangelicals, Reagan's "Evil Empire" is now no longer the USSR as a Communist power, but the former Soviet Union as a Muslim power. On the eve of the collapse, Evangelical ideologue Lester Sumrall wrote

Currently living in the lands of Magog, Rosh, Meshech and Tubal (southern Russian and modern Turkey) [Ezek. 38:3] are the largest concentrations of Muslims in the Soviet Union. The Islamic growth rate in these regions is five times that of the rest of the Soviet Union. The Soviet armed forces are currently made up of about 35 to 40 per cent Muslim troops. With Islamic motivation, revival and zeal sweeping the USSR and the Middle East, it is only a matter of time before Ezekiel 38:15-16 is fulfilled, partly by the Soviet Union's Muslim people.

Also taking part in the invasion of Israel prophesied by Ezekiel, Sumrall lists "Persia (Iran), Ethiopia, Libya, Gomer (southern USSR) and Togarmah (eastern Turkey)."[13] It is thus sometimes difficult to separate political and religious elements in the hostile attitudes expressed about the Middle East and the

Islamic World in various public fora.

Whatever their motivation, these notions are strikingly expressed on the cover of the May 1994 issue of *World Press Review* featuring an picture of two minarets silhouetted against the setting sun. On this scene is superimposed "Fear of Islam, Is it a real world menace, or just the latest evil empire?" implying that there are no other possible interpretations. The answer seems to be provided by the accompanying images.

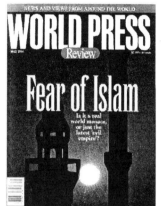

The third set of factors in conditioning images of the Other in general, and the Muslim Other in particular, is the unprecedented demographic reshaping of American society in the last several decades. Immigration from abroad now accounts for almost 30% - or nearly 1/3 - of US population growth with approximately 1 million legal and illegal immigrants arriving here annually. In comparison with previous demographic influxes, the nature of this immigration has fundamentally changed as well. Since 1960, the US immigrant population has increased by over 100%, but more than 80% of this increase has come from the so-called Third World as opposed to 4% from Europe. In 1990, moreover, 1 in 10 residents in the nations metropolitan areas was foreign born. In New York City, for example, 1 in 5 was foreign born, nearly 1 in 3 spoke a language other than English, and almost half of that number acknowledged that they do not speak it well. Finally, unlike previous patterns of immigration in which the newcomers settled mainly in the cites, the current wave has transformed American life from the largest urban centers to the smallest townships and remotest rural areas. Immigration from the Islamic World then fits squarely within these parameters.

The fourth factor is related to the profound contemporary changes in the US and world economies sometimes referred to as globalization. On the domestic level, in June 1996 the US Census Bureau reported on growing economic inequality in the US, stating that there now existed the widest gap between rich and poor since the end of World War II. Members of the American middle and lower classes have experienced a real decline in their standards of living and many have been the victims of downsizing during a period of unprecedented corporate profits and levels of executive compensation. The hardships and frustrations produced by these developments have caused some to seek situations or individuals to blame for their predicament. More often than not, the new immigrants, including Muslims, are the targets of their hostility.

All four factors - the shortcomings of US foreign policy, extremist religious ideologies, a rapidly changing demography, and the perception of economic inequity - have helped to create a negative social atmosphere elements of which range from a loss of civility through racism to the proliferation of hate crimes against minority ethnic, religious, and cultural groups. The attitudes underlying these elements are clearly documented in the National Conference survey mentioned above. In other words, alongside those threatening us from abroad, we seem to have discovered a number of enemy Others within . This prelude to self-destruction is one of the most serious challenges faced by the United States today.

MELTING POT, 1990

Payne
Scripps Howard

In his important exploration of the psychology of *homo hostilis*, Sam Keen states, "In the beginning we create the enemy. Before the weapon comes the image." He continues, "We *think* others to death and then invent the battle-axe or the ballistic missiles with which to actually kill them. Propaganda precedes technology."[14] In other words, much of what goes in to the construction of an enemy comes from within the human pysche. When a people or a society draw upon these inner resources, they tap into a reservoir of mental pictures to employ in the process of enemy making. "What we will find is that wars come and go, but strangely, amid changing circumstances - the hostile imagination has a certain standard repertoire of images it uses to dehumanize the enemy. In matters of propaganda, we are all platonists; we apply eternal archetypes to changing events."[15] If we accept Keen's thesis, then, images and stereotypes of the Middle East and the Islamic World are not only historically broad, but psychologically deep as well.

In establishing universal typology of enemy-making, Keen surveys political posters and editorial cartoons related to many different conflicts among many different peoples. The tropes and archetypes that he distinguishes in this process follow a consitent and predictable pattern ranging from the enemy as brute force to the enemy as vermin. The Middle East and the Islamic World naturally figure in the materials he studies, but only as occasional example of aspects of the process. In the following section, I will present examples illustrating these tropes as they relate principally to Islam and Muslims. It will be clear from these illustrations that American popular imagination has been conditioned to view Muslims as "the enemy" and Islam as the political and moral equivalent of Communism. It will be further apparent that these images are encountered in every segment of American culture: the press, journals of opinion, literature, electronic entertainment and news media, religious institutions, government, and education.[16]

## FACELESS HORDE, MINDLESS ENTITY, BRUTE FORCE

In his Ecclesiastical History of the English Nation, the Venerable Bede (735) described a 729 Muslim invasion of France as "a swarm of Saracens [who] ravaged Gaul." The same theme is echoed in popular news magazines today in vivid and emotive language:

> They jammed Revolutions Avenue in the heart of Tehran last week, a million Iranian raising their fists and shouting as if with one voice, "Revenge! Revenge! Revenge!" The clutches of women dressed in black chadors, the phalanxes of men bearing placards that said down with U.S.: the angry scene had been played out before. This time, however, the crowd seemed reinvigorated, its fury fresh and lethal. "Death to America! they chanted in the near 100° heat. Their rage rose higher still..."[17]

The following titles of articles and books preserve Bedes trope and carry it further: "Beware the Islamic Threat" (Yedidya

Atlas, *The Jerusalem Post International*, 14 March 1992); "The Islamic Wave" (Itamar Rabinovich, *Washington Quarterly* 2.4, August 1979; *The New York Times Magazine*, Judith Miller, 31 May 1992); "The New Islamic Whirlwind" (Ken Macqueen, *Macleans*, 1 April 1985); and "Fundamentalist Tidal Wave is Sweeping the Arab World" (Helen Davis, *Cleveland Jewish News*, 22 June 1990); and The "Green Peril:" *Creating the Islamic Fundamentalist Threat*, (Leon T. Hadar, Washington, 1992), to cite only a few. Enraged mobs and tidal waves are faceless, mindless, and overwhelming; they cannot be dealt with using normal measures or forms of rational discourse. Added to this now is that these entities can deploy the natural fury of the atom. Using the same frame of analysis, we do not seem to be as concerned that Christianity, Judaism, and Hinduism also have the bomb.

## VIOLENCE, IRRATIONALITY

That Islam is inherently violent is one of the most deeply embedded and persistent chestnuts in American and European anti-Islamic polemics. Along with the accompanying image, the following excerpts from an article by anthropologist

Raphael Patai, author of *The Arab Mind*, lamenting the assassination of Anwar Sadat appeared in the Chicago Tribune on December 12, 1981. According to Patai, this act represented the surfacing of "the darkest side of the Moslem-Arab personality" which thereby "gained momentary predominance over the many admirable qualities comprised in the Arab national character." I reproduce a large part of it as a virtual catalogue of the most common conceits and cliches about the alleged violence of Islam and the Muslims.

> The roots of the Moslem proclivity to settling differences with the dagger, the sword, the gun, or the bomb, either individually or in groups, go far back in Arab history...Feuding and intertribal warfare were age-old traditions in Arabia in the 7th Century, when Mohammed founded Islam and converted all the Arab tribes to his religion.
>
> As a result of the rapid expansion of Islam in the 8th century, Bedouin savagery was spread from Spain to India, infecting everyone who eventually accepted the new religion.
>
> ...The Arab proclivity toward conflict was exported to all the territories that became Arabized or at least Islamized, and it became a common feature of all Islamic peoples.

*Violence, the Islamic curse*

Patai emphasizes the role of violence and warfare in this early expansion:

At that early age, the *jihad*, the holy war against the infidels, was made a basic Moslem duty. To engage in a *jihad* was not merely a religious duty, but a collective obligation, because Islamic doctrine held in theory only Islam had a right to exist in the world, and hence had to be spread by the force of arms...The adage *Din Muhammad bilsayf* ["The Religion of Muhammad by the sword"], has for centuries been the resounding popular response given to the doctrine of *jihad* by people whose psyche has been formed by Islam...

After pointing to numerous examples of hostilities involving Muslim states between 1961 and 1981, Patai attempts to marshal historical precedent for this aggressive behavior.

...Sadat's assassination points up another traditional manifestation of the age-old Arab-Moslem proneness for conflict: The practice of eliminating a political or religious opponent by dispatching killers to murder him. Of the first four caliphs [632-61], three were assassinated, and ever since innumerable Moslem leaders have been felled by Moslem assassins' hands... assassination as such is more Middle Eastern than a Western mode of religious or political action. The very existence of the religious duty of *jihad*, despite all the limitations put on it by orthodox doctrine, is easily misinterpreted by the warped mind of the assassin as sanctioning his own personal act of war against his chosen target. In addition, the Moslem assassin is endowed with a greater recklessness, encouraged by a belief in predestination even without the use of hashish that enables him to act without being hampered by consideration for his own safety.

Arabs and by extension all Muslims are therefore universally endowed with a national character marked by a barely repressed tendency to resort to violence. The predisposition is reinforced by their religion which promises them paradise in return for spreading their faith by force.

In *The Lucifer Principle*, Howard Bloom picks up where Patai leaves off by offering an explanation of the origins of Islamic violence. Like Patai, Bloom begins with a series of generalities about Bedouin culture which he asserts is "the mother of all Islam" and Bedouins who "in their austere tents keep the true spirit of Islam alive." According to Bloom, moreover, they have remained unchanged over time so that Bedouin practices today are virtually the same as those of their ancestors 1,400 years ago. Bedouins, it seems, behave very harshly toward their children, showing them little or no affection. "Could," asks Bloom, "the denial of warmth lie behind Arab brutality?  Could that deprivation help explain their thirst for blood?"  The answer appears to be affirmative leading Bloom to view contemporary Arab (not Bedouin!) society as composed of individuals "thrust into a life of cold isolation" who have become "walking time bomb[s]."  He concluded by extending this perception to a whole civilization: "An entire people may have turned barbaric for the simple lack of a hug."[18]

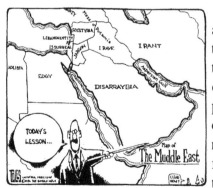

The idea that all Muslims are stamped with the negative traits of violence and irrationality is frequently expressed in editorial cartoons showing one part of the Islamic world or the other subdivided into units the names of which proclaim this fact. Such representations also tell us that understanding the region or its inhabitants is completely out of the question. Attempting to comprehend the incomprehensible and reasoning with madmen are utterly futile undertakings.

One particular type of violence, namely terrorism, has become inextricably linked with Islam and Muslims in the popular imagination. This linkage builds, moreover, upon the traditional Western misunderstanding of *jihad*, examples of which can be seen in some of the passages quoted above. In the following images, the identification of Islam and terrorism is explicit the Farrakhan figure is carrying a book called *Allah's Tidbits of Terror* and the door of the terrorists hideout is marked "Association of Moslem Terrorists."

Muslim Madman March

The Islamic Revolution in Iran also became a veritable goldmine for images associating what were thought to be "official" representatives of Islam with violence in such forms as the gun-toting mullah and the *jihad*-spewing ayatollah.

## BARBARIAN, SAVAGE

As a savage, irrational horde, Muslims are frequently stereotyped as a serious danger to Western cultural and religious traditions. Though Islam is an Abrahamic faith alongside Judaism and Christianity, it is usually seen as threatening both "mom and apple pie" as well as basic "Judeo-Christian values." In struggling against such people, then, we are not only protecting everything we hold near and dear in our own culture, but also in a sense we are continuing the "civilizing mission" of the European colonial powers referred to earlier.

## THE GREEDY, AVARICIOUS ENEMY

This trope is usually based on the assumption that the antagonist possesses an insatiatable appetite for domination over all natural resources and other forms of wealth, usurping the rights of its rightful owners, depriving legitimate consumers, and thereby undermining the economic well-being of the rest of the world. As mentioned above, the "oil boycott" of the 1970s helped create the impression that Arabs and other Middle Easterners, through organizations like OPEC, were trying to gain control of major oil reserves and use their enormous profits first to ruin and then to buy up the United States; rarely was it noted that countries like Great Britain, Canada, and the Netherlands held much larger shares in the American economy than any Middle Eastern or Islamic country.

In addition to gaining control of resources and real property, "Arabs" were also thought to be attempting to "buy" American lawmakers and other officials. In this connection, we need only recall Abscam, a 1978 FBI sting operation in which

IMPORTED OIL STRENGTHENS OUR TIES TO THE MIDDLE EAST.

alleged agents of a fictitious Arab "sheik" offered selected public officials money or other considerations in exchange for special favors. This operation eventually resulted in the indictment and conviction of one senator and four congressmen on charges of bribery and conspiracy. Today, the Arabs have largely been displaced in this role by the Japanese.

With the gradual fading of the threat of "petro-terrorism," a new economic and financial menace related to the Islamic world raised its head - the Bank of Credit and Commerce International. According to a 1992 article in the Wall Street Journal by Rachel Ehrenfeld, "...The aim of B.C.C.I., from the outset, was to put forward a radical-Islamic political agenda and to support third world causes. B.C.C.I.'s founder, Pakistani businessman Agha Hasan Abedi, a member of the ultra-religious, quasi-secret Sufi sect [*sic!*], made plain the bank's ideological bent. He and other bank officials openly discussed their political and religious mission which was nothing less than economic competition with and eventual domination of Western financial and political institutions. Through various underhanded means, B.C.C.I. bankrolled "all the Islamic fundamentalists as well as terrorist groups like Abu Nidal and Shining Path, the violent Maoist terrorist organization operating in Peru" along with those of "criminals, drug lords and the corrupt." Finally, Ehrenfeld expresses shock that governments allowed such a scheme to exist for almost two decades before shutting it down. Thus, not only is

Muslim financial power linked with violence and terrorism, but is it imagined as a sort of cancer on the world economy that may metastasize before it is recognized or diagnosed.

## DEMON, DEVIL

Demonization of the Other is the antithesis of the notion that "God is on our side." As Keen notes, "The Devil, like the God of politics, is essentially created to allow us to deny responsibility for our actions... Both God and the Devil seem to testify to the abiding human experience of being possessed by alien forces, being out of control, being unable to achieve autonomy."[19] This trope, then, is a variation on the "Evil Empire" theme introduced earlier.

Despite the recency of Reagan's rhetoric, Islam has been demonized for centuries in Western culture. For example, Dante Alighieri regarded Islam as the main force of the Antichrist in the world of his time and the very spirit of disorder and chaos. He consequently placed the Prophet Muhammad and his cousin and son-in-law Ali in the eighth circle of Hell as "sowers of scandal and schism."[20] A modern reprise of this medieval idea is found in a column by Jan Markell entitled "Islam is a Religion from Hell" published in *Twin Cities Newspapers*. After referring to atrocities allegedly carried out by "Shiite Moslems," Markell presents a brief, but distorted sketch of the rise of Islam and the career of the Prophet.

Mohammed knew his cause was worthless without converts. Here is where [the] modern-day Israel/Arab conflict began. The Jews refused to accept his new religion, so Mohammed resorted to what would become commonplace for the Moslems: eliminate the Jews by slaughter and banishment. He set a sordid example for his present disciples such as Gadhafi, Khomeini, Arafat, Assad, and more.

69

She then undertakes a comparison of Christianity and Islam: "Followers of Jesus are known, hopefully, by their love; the disciples of Allah and Mohammed are known for their cruelty and brutality. Islam gains followers through the edge of the sword. This has been true for centuries." The crux of her argument, however, occurs in the next paragraph.

Islam is a religion conceived in hell. It was and is determined to destroy all Jews and Christians. Again I refer to fundamentalist extremists. They are the ones who claim "holy war" upon an "unbelieving" world. Their "holy war" is inspired by Satan himself. The flames of holy war lenthen [sic] and strengthen as Satan senses the imminent arrival of the Messiah.

Though Markells diatribe places her among the fundamentalist-dispensationalist Christians discussed above, hers is certainly not the only voice demonizing Islam in the media and American popular culture.

## APOCALYPSE, DOOM, DEATH

The portrayal of the Other as death incarnate recalls the fact that conflicts are often seen in such Manichaean terms as Life vs Death, Black vs White, or Light vs Darkness. In these cosmic struggles, the Other as doom or bringer of death represents therefore the ultimate threat. Moreover, as Keen argues, "...propaganda must switch the blame for the massive suffering and death from us to them."[21]  In the second of the two images below, it is noteworthy that both the Pope and the "Moslem Fundamentalist" are shown in a hostile light because of their views on birth control and abortion, but the Pope is only caricatured while the Muslim is depicted as death.

## BEAST, REPTILE, INSECT

Imagining the Other as beast, reptile, insect, or microbe completes the course of dehumanization begun by constructing our enemies as violent, irrational subhuman barbarians. Such images provide the ultimate sanction for the extermination of the

The Descent of Man

*Levine/New York Times*

Other by conditioning us to kill without incurring guilt.[22]  It is often sufficient only to picture the enemy leader in this fashion, since, through reductionism everyone associated with him is similarly dehumanized - if Saddam Hussein is lower than a reptile, then the Iraqi people are certainly no better and deserved to be "bombed back into the Stone Age."

A final example is this social studies handout distributed for a number of years by a teacher in a suburban Chicago middle school. It is significant not only as a concluding summary of the enemy-making devices introduced in this section and their uniformity, but also as an indication of how widespread the process actually is.

# SOCIAL STUDIES HANDOUT
Junior High School, North Chicago Suburbs, 1987

Arabs Have Poverty Chaos, Disunity
Because they are:

Tribalistic
Egocentric
(society emphasized self)
Self Indulgent
Narrow in Outlook
Warlike
Violent
Intolerant
Spoiled
Undisciplined
Unprincipled
Petty
Immature
Cruel & Callous to Living
Things
Scornful of Work
Indifferent to Nature
Envious
Lustful
Greedy
Hateful
Disrespectful of Women as
Partners
Harsh, etc

These same cultural traits can be seen in Spain, Sicily, Central and South America due to the 700 years of occupation of Spain by the Arabs all on top of a system we know as asiatic despotism

With limited resources (same as Arabs*) The Israelis have constructed the strongest, most stable, most progressive, most democratic, most hopeful country in the Near East

Because they have the morale based on:

Self sacrifice
Self discipline
Social Solidarity
Readiness to Work
Cooperation
Hope for the Future

And are Devoted to

Science
Democracy
Individual respect
Technology

(All Western Traits)

All of the above have made them cursed and denounced by the Arabs whose hysterical hatred is not aimed at the loss of Palestine as a land but because of these qualities make the Arabs look bad today and for everything in their history they have been doing

*Except the Arabs have oil.
More in class as to why they have these traits.

The importance of education in dispelling ignorance, the breeding ground of prejudice, bias, and racism is beyond question. It is likewise clear, however, that any effort to educate that does not take into consideration the cultural, historical, and psychological factors discussed in this essay will probably achieve only limited success. It therefore behooves anyone wishing to impart accurate information on the Middle East and the Islamic World not only to master the material that he or she plans to deliver, but also to be aware of the context in which this material is to be presented. This applies to the classroom as well as to the town meeting.

At the end of its report on the 1993 poll on attitudes toward Islam, the American Muslim Council recommended that "American Muslims must become less isolated and become more involved in community affairs. American Muslims must also seek inclusion and increasing participation in ecumenical services and local projects." Surely there can be no doubt on this count either. Involvement - both individual and collective - will certainly begin to help prevent some of the outrages perpetrated against the Muslim community in the past. Active participation in monitoring the media and bringing matters of concern to the community to the attention of those accountable will go a long way toward showing journalists how to become more sensitive to those concerns. Taking part in Parent-Teacher Associations and other school-related organizations will also help protect Muslim and non-Muslim American children from exposure to the sort of ignorance and falsehood the consequences of which we have just discussed. Finally, activism in defending and strengthening our democratic political institutions will contribute to safeguarding the civil and political rights of the American Muslim community while gradually bringing it into the mainstream of American life.

Islam is now an American religion and has much to offer in its moral and ethical vision of society and its emphasis on sound family and community values. American Muslims are responsible for seeing that this vision and these values are integrated into our common heritage. Drawing on these internal sources of strength and power, perhaps we unlike the interlocutor in Cavafys poem *Waiting for the Barbarians* - can find solutions to political and social problems based on intelligence, righteousness, and compassion instead of allowing forces outside ourselves of which we are scarcely aware to impose settlements upon us.

[1] C. P. Cavafy ( 1933). "Waiting for the Barbarians," *Six Poets of Modern Greece*, trans. by Edmund Keely and Philip Sherrard (New York Alfred K. Knopf, 1961), p. 32.

[2] Walter Lippmann. *Public Opinion* (New York: Free Press, 1965; originally published 1922), p. 9; and cf. p. 57.

[3] Tom W. Smith. *What do Americans Think about Jews?* New York: American Jewish Committee, 1991 (*Working Papers on Contemporary Anti-Semitism*, no. 8).

[4] American Muslim Council, *American Attitudes toward Islam: A Nationwide Poll*. New York: American Muslim Council, [1993].

[5] The National Conference. *Taking Americas Pulse, A Summary Report of the National Conferences Survey on Inter-Group Relations*. New York, 1994.

[6] Council on American-Islamic Relations. *A Rush to Judgment*. Washington, 1995.

[7] Lippmann, *Public Opinion*, p. 158.

[8] Lippman, *Public Opinion*, pp. 63-64.

[9] See, for example, Norman Daniel, *Islam and the West, The Making of an Image* (Edinburgh: Edinburgh University, 1960).

[10] See Norman Daniel, *Islam, Europe, and Empire* (Edinburgh: Edinburgh University, 1966) and Edward W. Said, *Orientalism* (New York: Vintage Books, 1979).

[11] Wilfred Cantwell Smith, *Islam in Modern History* (Princeton: Princeton University Press, 1957)

[12] Samuel P. Huntington, "The Clash of Civilizations," *Foreign Affairs* 72 (Summer 1993), pp. 22-49. See the comments of Ralph Braibanti, *The Nature and Structure of the Islamic World* (International Strategy and Policy Institute: Chicago, 1995), pp. 13 ff.

[13] Quoted by Paul Gifford in "Islam as 'The Enemy,'" *The Tablet, The International Catholic Weekly* 244 (6 October 1990), p. 1261.

[14] Sam Keen, *Faces of the Enemy, Reflections of the Hostile Imagination* (Harper and Row: San Francisco, 1986), p. 10.

[15] Keen, *Faces*, p. 13.

[16] On the phenomenon of Arabophobia, see, for example, Laurence Michalak, *Cruel and Unusual: Negative Images of Arabs in American Popular Culture* (Washington, D.C.: American-Arab Anti-Discrimination Committee, Issue Paper 15, 3rd ed. 1988); Jack Shaheen, *The TV Arab* (Bowling Green, Ohio: Bowling Green State University Popular Press, 1984); and Janice Terry, *Mistaken Identity, Arab Stereotypes in Popular Writing* (Washington, D.C.: American-Arab Affairs Council, 1985).

[17] "At War on All Fronts," *Time*, August 17, 1987.

[18] Excerpted as "The Importance of Hugging," *Omni*, February 1989, pp. 30, 116.

[19] Keen, *Faces*, pp. 109-10.

[20] Dante, *Inferno*, Canto 28.

[21] Keen, *Faces*, p. 65.

[22] Keen, *Faces*, pp. 60-61.

# MUSLIMS IN THE USA
# OPPORTUNITIES AND CHALLENGES:
# A PROACTIVE VISION.[1]

*Javeed Akhter*
*Executive Director ISPI*

As illustrated by John Woods in the preceding article, although the mutual perceptions of Muslims and (for lack of a better term) of "The West" are flawed, Muslims are by and large the recipients of much of the misunderstanding and consequent stereotyping. One manifestation of this stereotyping, is the alarm academia, think tanks and popular media in the West have sounded in rather strident tones, that the "Muslims are coming."[2] The irony is that the Muslims are already here. Many families have three generations in this country and they are here to stay. Muslims are no longer the "other," or the "alien" living in some distant land. They are in the workplace, in the schools, and in the neighborhoods. As estimated by Asad Husain, there may be as many as six million Muslims in this country.[3] They are the second or the third largest religious group after Christians. They are clearly more numerous than many Christian denominations. To the chagrin of some they have not fulfilled the stereotype of the violent extremist followers of an exotic religion. These caricatures which television and movies use to portray Muslims are about as realistic as the characters on a day time soap opera. In fact, it is hard to recognize most Muslims as different from the mainstream. They go to work as anyone else, share the same anxieties and experience the same joys as everyone around them. By most objective standards, they are as law abiding, peaceful and productive members of the society as any other ethnic or religious group. They are therefore understandably bewildered and frustrated by the hostility directed against them by some sections of American society. Some of the causes of this hostility go far back into history, in particular the Crusades, and may take decades to change. Karen Armstrong in her book Muhammad: The Biography[4] addresses this issue comprehensively.

It should be noted that some of the negativism against Muslims is a consequence of their immigrant and minority status, not their faith. It is unusual for Western nations to have such large numbers of Muslims amongst them. In previous centuries when Muslims were in a minority, they were mostly the ruling class. A substantial proportion of Muslims today live in what has been called by Dr. Braibanti the "Darul-Muhajirin (the land of the immigrants)."[5] There are no clear precedents in Muslim history to deal with the challenges which this immigrant situation has created. It is essentially an uncharted territory which calls for creative solutions that are consistent with core Islamic beliefs.

Muslim immigrants in this country have generally superior levels of education and typically high standards of living. These characteristics raise special problems and dilemmas for those who nurture the old stereotype of "the backward Muslim." How can these "Barbaric Others,"[6] be so successful and prosperous? Why is there such a perceived differential in moral conduct between the followers of this "primitive and defeated" religion called Islam and "the modern and victorious West"? The differential in socio-economic status provokes jealousy and hostility. This type of xenophobia, although not uniquely directed against Muslims, (many Asians from the Far East are also the victims of this type of xenophobia), makes their task of adjustment even more difficult. However, "the Muslim next door," has also fostered, albeit on a modest scale, a discussion of pluralistic and inclusionary philosophy amongst non-Muslim religious scholars, moving away from the traditional doctrine of Christian Particularism.[7]

## CHALLENGES FOR MUSLIM AMERICANS

Occidentalism, a biased analysis of Western ideas and institutions, should not be the Muslim response against Orientalism, which is a prejudicial analysis of Islam by some Western scholars. Occidentalism will lead only to reverse racism. Another challenge for Muslims is to resist cynicism and not to get embittered by the objectively unfair treatment that they receive at the hands of the media. They must resist the understandable tendency towards self imposed isolation and avoid a retreat into the mosques and community centers. Moreover, if they isolate themselves, they will merely succeed in creating their own ghettos. They cannot ignore the problems around them, hoping to remain immune to them. Muslims must remember the Qur'anic injunction to be a people of knowledge, compassion, and patience, striving for positive change in the communities in which they live ("Amar bil Maruf wa Nahi Anal Munkar": enjoin good and prohibit wrong).[8] Meaningful changes must be initiated within themselves. Only then will they be respected and their example used as a precedent for others.

Not enough of the energy and enthusiasm shown by Muslims in performing the various religious obligations and rituals appears to translate into social or political activism. The Qur'an stresses that faith and righteous action should go together, as if they are two sides of the same coin (Aaminu wa Amilu Salihat: Believe and work righteously).[9] Additionally, it is necessary for Muslims to scrape off from the core faith, the cultural accretions which have accumulated over time. This would necessitate a moving away from their own version of particularism which comes from blind following of tradition (Taqlid) and leads to divisions within the community. It is the Muslim's near sacred duty to think, ponder and meditate, coming up with creative and open minded solutions for newly emerging problems. A number of activists and scholars have attempted this type of reform with varying degrees of success.[10]

For inspiration, Muslims may look to their own history, when they had the assurance and self confidence to assimilate freely alien ideas and cultures into their own and to incorporate knowledge in a positive and creative way. If they can achieve today the same kind of synthesis between Islamic ideals and modern ideas, as they successfully did in the past, they would once again help to make unique and memorable contributions to the society, possibly becoming its most productive and proactive members and a source of moderation. Creating the exemplary "moderate community", (Ummatan Wasta: the "moderate nation" as the Qur'an calls it)[11] is a goal that can be achieved by maintaining a positive attitude, and remaining engaged in the society, as well as following a proactive plan of action.

## CHALLENGES FACING NON-MUSLIM AMERICANS

Non-Muslim Americans dealing with Muslims face many daunting challenges as well. The most fundamental is to recognize that there is a deep seated problem in the manner in which most view Muslims, and to a lesser degree, other indigenous and immigrant minorities. Prejudice stems from ignorance, which in turn leads to fear and hostility. Automatically equating terrorists with Muslims is one example of the accumulation of this stereotyping. In reality, the Palestinian bomber is as representative of Islam as the IRA bomber is of Christianity or the Tamil bomber is of Hinduism. In fact, Islam consistently teaches respect for human life, social justice and family values. It abhors violence. The Qur'an equates the saving of a life to the saving of all mankind and the unjust taking of a life as a crime against all humanity.[12]

The widespread misinformation about Muslims is not just in the media but also in text books. It is exacerbated by the Eurocentric view of history, which is the normative way of learning in American text books.[13] There has to be a paradigm shift, replacing it with a more balanced rendering of history. These biases can change only with the acquisition of objective knowledge. This is already taking place in a modest fashion in the classroom. [14] A more balanced understanding of Muslims and Islam may lead to a true pluralistic future for this country.

Currently, pluralism seems to be limited to various Christian denominations and sensitivity to the Judaeo-Christian tradition. Muslims even though an integral part of the Abrahamic tradition (Judaeo-Christian-Islamic) are almost universally ignored. In fact it appears as if no one other than Christians and Jews live in this country.

The majority community in any nation has the duty and obligation to practice true pluralism, not just tolerance. In a multi-religious, multi-ethnic society like the US, there can be no alternative to pluralism, which is an essential ingredient in the infrastructure for nation building. As perhaps the biggest challenge, nation building requires courage, foresight, and a steadfast adherence to high ideals.

## WORKING TOGETHER TO BUILD THE "MODERATE NATION"

Working together with their countrymen, Muslims can make an invaluable contribution in the areas of social and economic justice and human rights. To strive for justice and the rights of the displaced and the dispossessed should be a Muslim's primary objective as it is indeed one of Islam's salient goals.[15] Islam places the pursuit of justice at a very high level in its value system.

A false sense of brotherhood or nationalism should not prevent anyone from speaking out against unjust practices, rulers, or countries. Having the courage to stand up for justice is a daunting, but indispensable, task. Muhammad (S)[16] urged Muslims to stop injustice actively, and at the very least not to rationalize it.[17] Any individual or group which challenges the status quo is inevitably perceived as a threat and becomes the target of vilification or worse. Muslims should be ready to take the lead and pay the difficult and demanding but honorable price of standing up for truth.

The following is an outline of a Muslim proactive vision of opportunities and concrete steps toward nation building, for all Americans working together.

## A PROACTIVE VISION

*Restoring Civility To Daily Life*

Muslims, along with other thoughtful people, should strive to restore civility in daily life- a lofty but necessary goal. Humanity has always been in need of divine wisdom and knowledge. The first step in obtaining this divine wisdom is for man to realize the limited nature of his capabilities and his lack of self sufficiency. Next he should seek solutions from transcendental sources and introduce them into everyday life. One small step in this direction would be to start the work and school day with a moment of silence. There should be a provision of time and space for individual prayers.

The harmful consequences of the general lack of civility in society results in dysfunctional homes, schools and workplaces. Moral behavior and conduct should be taught and practiced in schools, and a greater emphasis should be placed on discipline.

The home and not the school is of course the primary area for character building. Violence at home spills over into violence on the street. The epidemic of violence at home should be stopped by allocating resources, and providing help to emotionally needy families. In addition, parental responsibility may be enforced by holding parents accountable for their minor children's criminal behavior.

The marginalization of the elderly should stop. The state should provide support to allow the elderly to live at home with their family rather than spend the most lonely and vulnerable years of their lives in nursing homes.

*Alcohol, Drugs, Gambling and Illicit Sex*

Another symptom of a lack of a sense of purpose in society is its attitude towards alcohol drugs and illicit sex. No battle against drugs can be successful as long as society continues to tolerate the use of alcohol as a legitimate social drug. There should be as vigorous a campaign against alcohol as there is against drugs and cigarette smoking.

All gambling, including state sponsored lotteries, should be discouraged. The justification of using gambling revenues for education is mere hypocrisy, and teaches children values exactly the opposite of what they should learn. The means should always be consistent with the ends.

Every attempt should be made toward restoration of women's dignity in society by removing sexuality to the private domain. Current society trivializes women in all types of forums. Electronic and print media are probably the worst culprits. It should be recognized that men and women have equal but separate and complimentary roles. Premarital and extramarital sex should not be condoned and accepted. Sex education classes should emphasize the practice of abstinence as a primary value, underlining the potent destructive, emotional, and moral consequences of sex outside marriage. They should emphasize responsible behavior.

*Socio-Economic Justice*

The most important part of a fair civil structure is

socio-economic justice.[18] The richest country in the world is still poor if it cannot provide equity in the areas of education, and health care. Reasonable educational opportunities should be available to everyone who desires them. Less investment in arms and ammunition and more in books and computers is the only way to stay on top of the world. Alternatives should be provided to promote competition among schools and improvement of the quality of education without destroying the public school system. College education, in particular, deserves special attention. It is becoming so expensive that soon it will be out of the reach of most people.

Health care should be reformed in several major areas. There is a need for everyone to have a minimum of catastrophic coverage. There is also need for serious tort reform. This reform of the litigation system is needed in many areas, not just in healthcare.

Social justice cannot be accomplished without economic justice. This could be achieved by modifying the current banking system, which emphasizes interest bearing loans and deposits, to one based on a model with equal risk sharing. Risk sharing, which is a core ingredient of an Islamic economic system, provides the lender with a strong incentive to be sure he is supporting the right venture. As pointed out by many western economists many of the bank disasters of the seventies could have been avoided if this concept was practiced. Usury should be redefined more stringently.

A sense of accountability and compassion for the displaced and dispossessed should shape capitalism, not just market forces. Emancipation of the dispossessed and the homeless with programs designed to promote self reliance should be encouraged. Job protection, similar to the Japanese model, should be an essential part of the corporate culture even if it means accepting smaller dividends for the investor.

*Political Equity*

A socio-economically just society is possible only if it is governed by the honest and the truthful. Electoral processes should be based on issues and not on artfully created illusions. Negative campaigning should be highly discouraged and banned if possible. Many qualified individuals either do not run for office or decide to quit because of the energy they have to spend raising money, and countering lies and slurs. Far too much money is needed to run a political campaign most of which is spent on advertisements in the electronic media. Candidates should be given equal and free access to the media. The election process should be much shorter than it is now. The length of the current election process is disruptive to both domestic reform and foreign policy initiatives. Election reform should include stringent measures against lobbyists and special interest groups.

Our current democratic system is not functioning well for most minority groups and interests. Groups without money or clout are left out in the cold. Minorities, as defined by the federal statutes should be given special consideration on issues which primarily concern their religious or ethnic interests via the mechanism of "advisory bodies".

*A Just Judicial System*

A civil society presupposes equal justice for all. There appears to be different standard for the poor, the minorities and the disenfranchised. We should consider significantly modifying, the jury system in favor of legally trained, and not elected, judges. If politicians don't become judges, then judges will not play politics. Active measures should be taken to cut down law suits by triaging and providing mechanisms for out of court settlements.

As the Qur'an suggests, there is great wisdom in allowing victims or the relatives of the victims a voice in the sentence given to the criminal.[19] They should have the choice of forgiving the culprit or accepting restitution. There should be continued and vigorous protection of the rights of the individuals against the abuse of power by the law enforcers.

## Compassion for the Immigrants

A just society is a compassionate society. Illegal immigration should be firmly curtailed, but illegal immigrants should be treated with compassion. Legal immigration should be expanded to include the extended family. Immigration is the main reason why America has remained such an energetic and vibrant country for such a long time.

## A Just Foreign Policy

Foreign policy should be based on upholding justice rather than maintaining the status quo at any cost. Our country should be great enough to make national interest subservient to the larger ideal of human justice. Both individual and state terrorism should be condemned. State terrorism is a greater evil than the individual variety, for it is far more pernicious and destructive. Democratic movements should be supported in all countries whether the likely result is accession to power of groups in line with American foreign policy interests or not. The long term results of this support for legitimate democratic movements will always be beneficial to our country and to humanity.

## SYNOPSIS

Muslim Americans realize that most of their countrymen, like themselves, are against the mindless plunge into a valueless post-modernistic society.[20] Muslims share with most Americans the worry that the relentless onslaught of secular humanism appears to promote the diminishing of the transcendent. The traditional American ideals of equality of rights, freedom of expression, the right to work hard and prosper, and the sanctity of the home, are values which Muslims also cherish deeply and consider to be essentially Islamic values. Everyone, except some of the entertainment media types, hate public indecency and the attrition of common civility. Everyone, including the entertainment types, hate crime and lack of accountability in society. These and many other areas of common values and complementary ideals should allow Muslims to work together as Americans in building a better society, the "Moderate Nation".

Muslims have a vision of the US, where there is a paradigm shift in emphasis from "individual rights" to "duties and obligations." The Muslim vision is of a nation which is mature and genteel: a nation which is cognizant of the enormous power it has, and wields it with responsibility. A nation which is able to avoid the mistakes arrogant nations made throughout history. A nation which is willing to be both the moral leader of the world and an economic and military super power. A moderate nation, which has restored civility to daily life, judges people only by their righteous actions and not by religion, social status, race, or gender. A nation which is generous in helping the displaced, the dispossessed and the needy and is always ready to uphold justice, remaining steadfast and patient in moments of peril.

There is much in our country which is good and exemplary and needs to be preserved. However, there is also much which needs to be altered and improved upon. As we straddle the millennia, it is critical to go through self appraisal and self criticism to be able to launch into an exemplary future. Some of the concepts proposed in this manifesto are new, and others are a reconfirmation of old ideals. Muslims in this country eagerly await opportunities to join the national debate and discussion, to participate in nation building and to enrich this country with the values which they have in their own unique and rich tradition.

[1] I gratefully acknowledge the efforts of all the scholars and ISPI members who helped in this effort. In particular I would like to acknowledge the efforts of my daughters Nausheen and Sabreen.

[2] "The Muslims are coming; The Muslims are coming." Headline on the title cover of the National Review. November 19, 1990.

[3] Asad Husain, "Muslim Demographics". Earlier article in this book.

[4] Karen Armstrong. "Muhammad, The Biography". The chapter titled Muhammad The Enemy, describes the historical misrepresentation and misconceptions with great accuracy and insight.

[5] Ralph Braibanti. "The Nature And Structure Of The Islamic world", published by ISPI in 1995.

[6] Zia Sardar. "Barbaric Others"; Pluto Press. London 1993.

[7] Christian Particularism implies the only truth to be salvation through Christ. All other belief systems are therefore considered false.

[8] Qur'an Chapter 3: Verse 110. Islam exhorts Muslims to take an active role in reforming society. It urges Muslims to establish good and stop evil.

[9] Qur'an. The phrase " Believe and work Righteously" appears numerous times in the Qur'an. Righteous has a very broad meaning in the Islam. It implies purity of soul, chastity, love, truth, respect for covenants, justice, patience and forbearance.

[10] Ann Marie Schimmel. "Islam"; An Introduction"; see chapter on the modern developments inside Islam. Publisher State University Of New York Press: Albany 1992.

[11] Qur'an Chapter 2: Verse 110. Dr. Syed Abdul Latif discusses this concept very well in his book " The Mind Al-Qur'an Builds"; Publisher Idarah Adbiyat, Delhi India.

[12] "Utne Reader". Special issue on Islam March/April 1994; pages 75-95.

[13] K. Y. Blankenship has published extensively on this subject. Some of the articles have appeared in the Journal of Islamic social sciences published by IIIT.

[14] Shabir Mansuri's project; The Council of Islamic Education, based in of California is doing remarkable work in correcting erroneous writings on Islam in school text books.

[15] M. M. Pickhtall. "Cultural Side Of Islam"; Publisher Kitab Bhavan, Delhi, India. The author quotes extensively from the Qur'an an d Hadith including the saying of Muhammad (S) " He is not with us who sides with his tribe in injustice -- ". Qur'an 5:8 "for the sake of God stand up to uphold justice and let not ill will toward any people impel you to deviate from justice.---this is indeed akin to piety--. Also see 4:135 6:153 of the Qur'an.

[16] (S); short for the Arabic phrase " *Sallal Lahu Alaihi Wasallam*" which means " Peace be upon him".

[17] Muhammad's (S) saying recorded by Bukhari in his book of Hadith.

[18] Fazalur Rahman. "Islam And The Problem Of Economic Justice"; Pakistan Economics, August 24: 1979.

[19] Qur'an. Chapter 2: Verse 178. Qur'an allows capital punishment for murder. However it encourages relatives of victims to forgive the perpetrator. The relatives may accept money in resti-

tution as long as it is done with a fair and generous intent.

[20] Akbar S Ahmed. "Post Modernism And Islam". Publisher Routledge, London 1992.

# ABOUT ISPI

The International Strategy and Policy Institute (ISPI) was established in 1994 by a group of American Muslims in the Chicago area. Its objective is to promote the correct understanding about Islam in the United States. Also, it seeks to explain the moral ethical positions of Islam, by bringing those positions to bear on the formulation of public policy. The Institute is motivated by the belief that great nations like the United States should not just have interests but ideals. Islamic ideals promote justice and advocate a middle of the road approach.

One of the means of achieving these ideals is the publication of position papers on selected topics of public policy in which Islamic solutions might play a constructive role. The Nature and Structure of the Islamic World by Dr. Ralph Braibanti, James B. Duke Professor of Political Science Emeritus at Duke University, was the first position paper. Since publication in 1995, it has been mailed to over 900 individuals and placed on the library shelves of several selective universities, including: the University of Chicago, Duke, Northwestern, MIT, Columbia University, UCLA, etc. The Library of Congress and the State of Illinois Library also hold copies of the essay. Professors William Laurie of the University of South Florida, John Hunwick of Northwestern University, and Ghada Talhami of Wake Forest Academy have already incorporated it into their curricula for the upcoming school year. The position paper has also been acknowledged by numerous politicians and policy makers, including President Bill Clinton and the Prime Minister of Malaysia, Mahathir Mohammed. ISPI hopes to continue to build on this initial success in subsequent papers, dealing with issues about justice, the environment, family values, personal health, spiritual life and relations between Islam and other religions, particularly Judaism and Christianity.

# ABOUT THE AUTHORS

## Dr. Asad Husain

*Dr. Asad Husain* is a Professor of Political Science and Director of the Summer Institute of Islamic Studies at Northeastern Illinois University as well as President of the American Islamic College in Chicago. Before coming to Chicago in 1969, he taught at Minnesota State University in Winona, Minnesota, and at Kansas State University in Pittsburgh, Kansas. He received his Master of Arts degree in Journalism and International Relations and later went on for his Doctorate at the University of Minnesota. He has authored several books and articles.

In 1975 he established the Institute of Muslim Minority Affairs at King Abdul Aziz University in Jeddah, Saudi Arabia while serving as a visiting scholar. For his work on Muslim minorities, Husain received a Professional Advancement and Merit award in 1995 from Northeastern Illinois University.

He is one of the founders of the Muslim Community Center of Chicago and is affiliated with many other Islamic organizations.

In April of 1996, Carlo Cardinal Furno of Rome presented him with the Order of Merit by the Knights and Ladies of the Equestrian Order of the Holy Sepulchre of Jerusalem.

*Imran Husain* is a graduate student in Journalism and media, Chairperson of the Muslim Students Association at Michigan State University.

## Dr. John Woods

*Dr. John Woods* is a professor of Middle Eastern History in the department of History and Near Eastern Languages and Civilizations at the University of Chicago. He obtained his Ph.D from Princeton University in Near Eastern Studies. His academic honors include Fulbright Fellowship in1960 , Woodrow Wilson Fellowship in 1960-62 , Senior Research Scholar in Uzbekistan in 1979 and Research Fellowship at American Research Institute in Turkey in 1987-88.

Professor Woods is a member of numerous Professional Associations including American Council for Collaboration in Education and Language Studies, American Friends of "Oasis Of Peace", American Institute of Iranian Studies and Council of International Studies.

Professor Woods has published numerous articles and monographs  and has translated many books. He has taught courses in Islamic Civilization,  Islamic History, Persian Paleography and Diplomatics.

### *Dr. Javeed Akhter*

*Dr. Javeed Akhter* is a medical doctor.  He is the head of the Section of Pediatric Pulmonology at Hope Children's Hospital in Oak Lawn, IL. and is also on the faculty of the University of Illinois Medical School.  For his outstanding service and commitment to his work, Dr. Akhter was named the Faculty/Teacher of the Year in 1994-95.

Dr. Akhter is the Executive Director of ISPI.  He is also actively involved in a number of other Muslim organizations and is a published author.

ISPI's first publication *The Nature and Structure of the Islamic World* is available through the Institute. This publication has a long and highly rated essay by Professor Ralph Braibanti, James B. Duke. Professor of Political Science Emeritus, Duke University. It has an Afterword on the quintessentials of Islamic belief system by Javeed Akhter.

It may be obtained by calling or writing to ISPI:

ISPI
1211 West 22nd Street, Suite 408
Oak Brook, IL 60521
Telephone (630) 571-1600
Facsimile (630) 573-4848